COLLECTORS GUIDEBOOKS

John Smart

Daphne Foskett

JOHN SMART

THE MAN AND HIS MINIATURES

CORY, ADAMS & MACKAY

Dedicated to the memory of
THE LATE ARTHUR JAFFÉ

© 1964 by Daphne Foskett
FIRST PUBLISHED BY CORY, ADAMS & MACKAY LTD
39 SLOANE STREET, LONDON SW1
THE TEXT IS SET IN 'MONOTYPE' EHRHARDT
PRINTED AND MADE IN ENGLAND BY
W. & J. MACKAY & CO LTD, CHATHAM

Contents

⌐◦❍◦⌐

List of Illustrations

COLOUR PLATES
Illustrations are numbered left to right from the top

FRONTISPIECE

PLATE TWO *(facing p xiv)*

PLATE THREE *(facing p 30)*

MONOCHROME PLATES (page 101)

All the portraits illustrated are finished miniatures on ivory unless otherwise stated. Those described as sketches were almost certainly studies for miniatures, but some are completed portraits on paper for many of which no finished miniatures can be traced. In a few cases it has not been possible to obtain measurements. An asterisk is placed against those which for varying reasons the author has been unable to inspect.

List of Illustrations

4
6
5
7

PLATE TWO

Preface

I T I S tantalizing that over two hundred years after John Smart's birth so little information is available about his life and background. For many years now he has been acknowledged to be one of the greatest exponents of miniature painting of the eighteenth century. His great contemporaries, Cosway, Engleheart, Humphry, and Plimer, have all been dealt with at some length by various authors, and their history is well known to students of miniature painting.

A volume on the life of Smart has been long overdue, and the reason for its omission has not been lack of interest, but the difficulty presented by lack of material. No diaries or fee books have so far been discovered, nor can his family be traced in spite of exhaustive inquiries in parish records, county files, and other documents.

The late Mr Arthur Jaffé spent many years' research on the life of this artist whose work he greatly admired, with a view to publishing a *catalogue raisonné*, a work which he was not, unfortunately, spared to complete. Such a work would now be almost impossible, owing to the difficulty of tracing the whereabouts of Smart's miniatures, which are scattered throughout the world.

Mr Michael Jaffé, with the consent of the rest of his family, kindly placed all his father's research at my disposal in the hope that I might continue the work which his father had begun. I have been able to add considerably to the initial material, and although there are still details that have eluded me, I feel that sufficient data has been found to make this monograph worth while.

As will be seen in the ensuing chapters, Smart's family history is rather complex and his private life somewhat different from that previously recorded.

I hope that this work will be of interest and assistance to collectors and students of miniatures, and will fill a gap in the history of miniature painting.

I should like to record my thanks to the innumerable people who have helped me so willingly with my research, and I am deeply indebted to those who have allowed me to reproduce miniatures from their collections.

I have been unable to trace the owners of certain illustrations which were collected by Mr Arthur Jaffé, and in these cases I would wish to apologize to any owners who have been omitted in my acknowledgements.

In particular I wish to thank Mr Michael Jaffé, Mrs Kahn, Miss Felicity Jaffé, and Mr Peter Jaffé for placing this material at my disposal and for encouraging me to write this book, and Mr J. W. Busteed, who provided me with invaluable Smart family papers.

My thanks are also due to many people who allowed me access to their collections. I am particularly indebted to the late Sir Bruce Ingram, Lord Wharton, Mrs Burton Jones, Mr and Mrs J. Starr, Mr A. G. Tite, Captain E. Woollett, and Mr E. Payne. Messrs Sotheby and Company and Messrs Christie, Manson and Woods Ltd, have been unfailing in their assistance. Mr R. W. Lewis of Gidea Park College, kindly allowed me access to the house and grounds.

Mr Graham Reynolds of the Victoria & Albert Museum has given me continued help and advice and I am also indebted to the Royal Academy, The British Museum, the Scottish National Portrait Gallery, the Royal Society of Arts, Commonwealth Relations Office, Somerset House and Messrs Coutts & Co. for permission to inspect material and records.

Mrs Dampier, Mr P. J. Williams and Miss D. M. Kleinfeldt helped with the initial sorting of the material and Mr J. Cecil, Miss C. Wolfe and Mr A. J. B. Kiddell, among others, have read the manuscript.

Miss S. Macnaughton and my daughter Helen helped to compile the index. Messrs A. C. Cooper (of London) have as always taken the greatest care in photographing many of the miniatures.

CHAPTER ONE

Early Life

FOR SOME time past the name of John Smart has figured prominently in the sale catalogues of portrait miniatures, and works by him have become costly. The eighteenth century was the heyday of miniature painting; artists worked hard to keep up with the demands of their patrons, and it was inevitable that some of them, because of the excellence of their work or distinguished patronage, should have received immediate recognition. Richard Cosway, George Engleheart, and Andrew Plimer were among those who enjoyed undoubted success throughout their careers, and their reputation has not diminished with the years. Others, however, did not make such an impact on the art critics of their time, but have since been given a much higher place in the estimation of those who have studied the subject.

John Smart is one whose work has come into greater prominence during the past fifty years and who now ranks as one of the greatest, some would say the greatest, of the eighteenth-century miniaturists. His portraits command exceedingly high prices and those who have examples of his miniatures in their collections consider themselves fortunate. That he was an outstanding draughtsman is evident to anyone who has had the opportunity of studying his work, for apart from the exquisite colouring and fineness of execution, his miniatures portray the characters of his sitters in a remarkable way. Unlike many of his contemporaries, no diaries or records have been discovered from which to piece together the story of his life, and in spite of years of research nothing is known about his birth, parentage or early education. It has always been alleged that he was born near Norwich, in the county of Norfolk, and early authors give the date of his birth as about 1740[1] or 1 May 1741,[2] but in spite of

---

[1] Redgrave, *Dictionary of Artists*, 1878, p. 398.

[2] Williamson, *Portrait Miniatures*, 1897, p. 49. *The History of Portrait Miniatures*, 1904, p. 2.

exhaustive inquiries in the area, no evidence to support this theory has so far been forthcoming, although family correspondence shows that his descendants are all convinced of the truth of the assertion that Norfolk was his birthplace.

There were some families of the name who lived in the parishes of Welney and Hilgay, villages not very far away from each other and within a few miles of Downham Market in Norfolk, and on 3 December 1741, John and Edward Smart, sons of George Smart, were baptized at Welney. On 30 November 1742, John, son of Edward and Mary Smart, was baptized at Hilgay. It is possible that one of these entries records the baptism of the artist, but so far it remains unproved.

It has been said that Smart's parents were married in St Peter's Mancroft, Norwich, and that he was born in 1742/3, but the registers of that church do not contain any such entry. Farington in his diary for 1809 records that on 5 August he met Smart, who 'mentioned Cosway as being a year older than himself, Cosway said he is 69' (Greig Edit.),[1] (67 in the typescript at Windsor Castle),[2] 'but he would have it believed that he is younger'. If Smart's statement was correct, he would have been born in 1742/3, which accords with the entry in the *Gentleman's Magazine* of June 1811, where it is stated that Smart at his death on 1 May was in his seventieth year,[3] whilst Cansick's *Monumental Inscriptions* relating to St James's Burial Ground, Hampstead Road, St Pancras, Middlesex, says that he died on 1 May 1811, aged 69 years.[4] This again points to the date being between 1742 and 1743.

In 1754 the Society of Arts decided to hold its first competition in London, and this provides the earliest evidence of Smart's existence, for he, together with Richard Cosway and others, entered for the section offering premiums for the best drawings by children under 14. The entries were to be submitted by 15 January 1755: the first prize was won by Richard Cosway and the second prize of £4 went to John Smart. The pencil drawing of a nude male figure posing as a river god, which gained him this success, was found within recent years in a folder with other drawings, in one of the Society's cellars.[5] It shows that even at an early age he possessed extraordinary powers of draughtsmanship.

[1] *Farington Diary*, Greig Edit., Vol. V, p. 217.
[2] *Farington Diary*, Windsor Typescript.
[3] *Gentleman's Magazine*, 1811.
[4] St Pancras Town Hall.
[5] Hudson and Luckhurst, *The Royal Society of Arts*, London, 1954; facing p. 47.

On the awards Cosway is noted as being 12 years old, and Robert Dossie in *Memoirs of Agriculture* says that Smart was under 12 when he entered.[1] The following are the awards received by Smart from the Society of Arts:

1755 2ND PRIZE FOR A NUDE MALE FIGURE OF A RIVER GOD.

1756 1ST PRIZE—A FIGURE STARTLED BY A RISING SERPENT.

1757 1ST PRIZE—PORTRAIT IN CHALK OF WILLIAM SHIPLEY.

1758 1ST PRIZE—A DANCING FAUN. (Class for under 18 years of age.)

The first two of these drawings and the fourth were among those found in the folder and are now in the Library of the Royal Society of Arts; the whereabouts of the portrait of Shipley is unknown. In each case Smart's draughtsmanship is superb and he had obviously made a close study of anatomy. It is interesting to note that whereas Cosway's name appears in the lists of awards for several years, Smart's name never appears again after 1758.

Both Cosway, on 19 August 1755, and Smart, on 23 September of the same year, were apprenticed to William Shipley (1714–1803), whose drawing school in St Martin's Lane attracted a large number of the young artists of the day. Both artists drew portraits of Shipley, and Cosway's, in oils, was presented by him to the Society of Arts in 1785.

In 1762 Smart, who at that time gave his address as Dean Street, Soho, first exhibited with the Society of Artists. This Society had sprung up from a small group of artists—chiefly foreign, who had experienced difficulty in obtaining models to sit for them. The group was conducted principally under the leadership of Mr Michael Moser, R.A. (1704–83) and met at first in an apartment in Greyhound Court, Arundel Street, removing later to Peter's Court, St Martin's Lane, where they were established in 1739. In the same year the Foundling Hospital was granted a charter, and later new buildings were erected. There was insufficient money to cover the cost of decorations and the rooms would have looked exceedingly bare but for the generosity of a number of artists who presented portraits and landscapes to overcome this deficiency. The Hospital authorities were so delighted with these acquisitions and grateful to the persons concerned that they opened their doors to the public and the Foundling Hospital soon became a popular resort. As a result of this success, artists conceived the idea of holding exhibitions of

[1] Dossie, R., *Memoirs of Agriculture*, Pub. 1768, 1771, and 1782, Vol. 3, p. 393.

their work, and it was felt that if this could be arranged annually, under the auspices of some society connected with the arts, it might well meet with success.

Among the information discovered in the papers now at the Royal Academy, connected with the Society of Artists of Great Britain, is an entry relating to this project—'At a meeting held at the Turk's Head Tavern, Gerrard Street, Soho, on 12th November, 1759, it was resolved to hold an Annual Exhibition of artists' work in the second week of April.'

The Society of Arts, Manufacture and Commerce, renamed 'The Royal Society of Arts' in 1908, which had been formed under the leadership of William Shipley in 1754, was an obvious choice. It possessed rooms large enough for the purpose, and the loan of its premises in the Strand was requested for the first exhibition, which was to be held from 21 April to 8 May, 1760. No charge for admission was permitted, and a compromise was made by selling catalogues at 6*d*. After a disagreement with the Society of Arts over the question of charges being made for admission, the Society of Artists of Great Britain held a rival exhibition in 1761 in Spring Gardens, Charing Cross, at which catalogues were sold for a shilling. This Society obtained a Royal Charter on 26 January 1765 as 'The Incorporated Society of Artists of Great Britain', and had at one time a membership of 211, which included the majority of the well-known artists of the day.

Among the papers relating to the Society of Artists is a minute book containing the details for the annual dinners, which were held on St Luke's Day. The plan of the tables is amusing and gives an idea of the type of menu and cost of such an affair.

Some artists who continued with the Society of Arts formed themselves into the Free Society of Artists. Inevitably a dispute arose among the members, and in 1765 the Free Society broke away from the Society of Arts and exhibited for two years in Maiden Lane, Covent Garden, and later used Lambe's Auction Rooms in Pall Mall. These exhibitions were not very successful and the Society came to an end in 1783. In the meantime the Society of Artists had also been having to contend with its own problems. At a meeting held on 19 February 1765, Smart was among the twenty-seven who were elected Fellows. He evidently took his responsibilities seriously, and from the records preserved is shown to have been not only an active supporter of the Society throughout its existence, but one whose advice and judgement was frequently taken. He rarely missed a meeting while he was in England, and his name often appears in the minutes in connexion with the Society's business.

In March 1765 'it was decided that no pupil or person under the age of 21 can be proposed as a Fellow of the Society. If any Fellow neglects to exhibit within the Society for two successive exhibitions he shall no longer be summoned to their meetings until he revives his claim for re-exhibiting.'

A great deal of controversy and unpleasantness ensued between the various societies and this eventually led to the formation of the Royal Academy, which opened its first exhibition in Lambe's Auction Rooms, Pall Mall, in 1769, under the Presidency of Sir Joshua Reynolds, who was knighted that year.

In 1771 Smart was made a Director of the Incorporated Society of Artists, which, in the same year, purchased land near the Exeter Exchange, in the Strand, with a view to building its own premises. On 16 July at a meeting of the Building Committee, which had been formed to deal with the project, it was agreed that the first stone should be laid 'on Saturday next . . . 1771'. The cost of maintaining these premises, once they were completed, was so great that the Society was soon in severe financial difficulties, and Smart, being concerned about the situation, offered assistance. On 21 October 1773 'it was resolved to accept Mr Smart's offer to lend the Society £100'.

On 29 October 1773, twenty-seven members agreed not to exhibit with any other Society for seven years, and on 22 March 1774 a further agreement was signed by some fourteen members, including Thomas Jones, binding them under a penalty of £100 for three years 'to exhibit in the same manner as heretobefore and not elsewhere'. This was no doubt an effort to prevent exhibitors from showing at the Royal Academy. The Incorporated Society of Artists was going through a difficult time, not only due to the financial strain, but also to differences of opinion among its members on other matters.

At a General Meeting held in the Society's Rooms on 31 March 1774, the financial difficulties were discussed and the following entry is of great interest—'Mr Smart and Mr Tassaert have voluntarily offered their security to the creditors of the Society to see their debts discharged in 3 years out of the profits of the four ensuing Exhibitions, together with the rents of the Society's Estate.' The members evidently accepted this offer, for at a General Meeting Extraordinary held in their Rooms on 2 June 1774, a Bond of Indemnity to Mr Tassaert and Mr Smart was signed, and also a bond of £100 penalty to exhibit with this Society and no other for three years.[1]

[1] Incorporated Society of Artists' papers now in the Royal Academy.

Algernon Graves refers to a letter in his possession written by six members of the Society, including Smart, which reads as follows:

To Monsieur George Romney

February 10th 1775
Sir,

We, the Committee of correspondence appointed by the Incorporated Society of Great Britain, with pleasure inform you that the difficulties we have hitherto laboured under are happily at an end; that peace and harmony are perfectly restored among us.

That the Society have made good their first payment with their creditors, at the close of the last Exhibition, and by the most moderate estimate, find, they shall be able to discharge the whole arrears, by Rents, and Profit of three succeeding Exhibitions, when we shall make a saving between six and seven hundred pounds per Annum, and have the satisfaction of being Posses'd of the best Exhibition Room in the Kingdom.

There is the greatest unanimity and spirit in the Society; all the principal Members have Voluntarily entered into an obligation for the support of the Society's credit, binding themselves in the penalty of an hundred pounds to Exhibit to their utmost till the debts incurred by the building are discharged.

Notwithstanding the absence of many of our Valuable Exhibitors, and the difficulties we then laboured under, we can with confidence affirm, we made a very respectable show.

The Society has entered into a resolution to purchase Frames of different sizes, to accommodate those Exhibitors who are unprovided.

The Exhibitions in future will open on the 23rd of April, and we are desired to request you will forward to us, as soon as possible, such of your works as you intend for Exhibition.

Among many regulations for securing the peace and concord of the Society, a Law has Pass'd that no President shall hold their chair for two successive years, but may be elected the third.

Peace being restored, our Property secured, in the quiet Possession of our Estate, and having the addition of several Valuable Fellows, Viz., Messrs. Brompton, Tate, Sykes, etc., with the assistance of Your works, doubt not but we shall make a very Capital Exhibition, and you may depend on the greatest care and attention to arrange them to the best advantage.

We are, Sir,
Your very humble Servts.

JNO. MORTIMER
S. GILPIN
JOHN DIXON
F. WHEATLEY
JOHN SMART
WM. MARLOW.

In spite of this eloquent letter, it is sad to relate that Romney did not send any pictures to the Exhibition.[1]

[1] Graves, *The Society of Artists and the Free Society*, London, 1907, pp. 324 and 325.

Although the Incorporated Society of Artists gained the support of a large number of people, it did not succeed in holding its own, or becoming financially solvent; consequently, it was resolved at a further meeting of the executive in 1776 that 'in view of the financial position there was no alternative but the sale of the premises in the Strand'. A committee was formed for this purpose, Smart being one of its members, and arrangements were accordingly made for the property to be sold by Mr Christie in three lots.

The estate was described in the following terms:

I. A Spacious and Capital Exhibition Room of the Royal Incorporated Society of Artists of Great Britain, situated in that Broad and commodious part of the Strand, near Exeter Exchange;

II. Likewise a Genteel House, occupying the same eligible situation adjoining the Approach to said Room; The Extensive Piece of Vacant Ground, immediately behind and contiguous to the same;
and also

III. Three Brick Messuages, Abutting thereon, and in Front of Exeter Street.

The sale was to take place on Friday, 26 July, at one o'clock.

At a meeting of the Society on 10 July 1776, it was proposed by Smart 'that their common seal be affixed thereto' on the letters of attorney, empowering the committee to dispose of the estate.

On 25 July 1776 the committee responsible for selling the estate met, the following being present—Tassaert, Parsons, Smart, Steuart, and Taylor. It was resolved at this meeting that a sum of not less than £4,700 should be accepted, although an entry in an earlier minute mentions £3,800. On 26 July 1776 the estate was duly put up for auction by Mr Christie and sold to a Mr Turner of Birmingham for £4,470. This is recorded at the General Quarterly Meeting of the Society on 3 September 1776, when the President reported that 'the Society's Estate sold for £4,470 to Mr Turner of Birmingham and that the Society's Mortgagee be informed, and the principal paid at three months as promised'. On 28 September that year it was agreed by the committee to notify the society concerned of their intention to pay off the mortgage on the estate of £3,000 on 24 December; Messrs Tassaert, Parsons, Smart, Steuart, and Taylor being present.

On 18 October 1777, at a meeting of Directors and Fellows held at the Crown and Anchor Tavern, in the Strand, Smart was elected a Director and Vice-President of the Society, and in the following year, on 19

October, at a meeting held at Foxe's Tavern, Bow Street, Covent Garden, he was elected President.

A medal bearing his portrait, modelled by Joachim Smith and cut by John Kirk, of which there are several versions, was struck in 1777, no doubt to celebrate the year he became Vice-President. At least two silver medals are known to exist, one engraved on the back 'September 22, 1798'. Several were struck in bronze, one in my own collection having 'Sarah Neale' engraved on the reverse, and at least one has come to my notice made of a silver alloy. When Smart's term of office as President expired he was succeeded by Richard Brompton (d. 1782), who was elected at a meeting of the Society at Foxe's Tavern on 18 October 1779. A portrait of Smart by Richard Brompton still exists, and is in the collection of Mr and Mrs John Starr of Kansas City.

From 1784 to 1789 the Society held no exhibitions at all, and after two more unsuccessful attempts in 1790 and 1791, it faded out. There are no records that give the details of the winding up of the Society, nor of the financial position after the sale of the estate, so that it has not been possible to discover the truth of the allegation that Smart lost money on the affair. From the information gained after a lengthy perusal of the papers relating to the matter, it is quite evident that Smart did all he could to encourage the Society and give it his financial support.

In the Royal Academy lists for 1784 there are two entries which have always been attributed to John Smart, but it is doubtful if they were by him. The entries were two pictures, not miniatures, and the address given as 39 Davies Street, Berkeley Square, and not Berners Street, which was Smart's address from 1765. Algernon Graves, in his works published in 1905–6 on the Royal Academy of Arts, lists these entries under John Smart, Junior, which is unlikely, as in 1786 he was only 8 years old.[1] Graves was unaware of this when he was writing, and thought John Junior was the son of Smart's first marriage. He did, however, alter these entries in *The Society of Artists and the Free Society*, and re-attribute them to John Smart, Senior.[2] They were in all probability by one of the other John Smarts who were artists.

It has been known for some time that several other artists of this name existed. It may well be that one of them also had a son, John Junior, who exhibited at the Royal Academy, and this has led to the erroneous conclusion that the entries recorded were by the son of John Smart, the miniaturist, whereas they were by a totally different artist.

[1] Graves, *The Royal Academy of Arts*, Vol. VII, p. 161.
[2] Graves, *The Society of Artists and the Free Society*, p. 236.

It has always been said that Smart was a member of a strict religious sect called Sandemanians or Glassites, but no trace of his name can be found among the records from 1766 to 1778 or from 1783 onwards. Dr Williamson, in a letter written on 7 November 1941 to Mr A. Jaffé, says he had no doubt in his mind that the information he gave on the subject in his book *Portrait Miniatures* was correct, and that even if Smart was not on the books of the Sect, he was at one time in sympathy with them, and worshipped at Barnsbury Grove or possibly one of their other chapels. It is quite evident from the details of his life as now known that he strayed far from their teaching concerning second marriages.

The name of his first wife is unknown, but the marriage must have taken place when Smart was a young man, and three children were born to them, John (b. 1762, who died young), Anna Maria (1766–1813), and Sophia (1770–93).

Mrs Smart later eloped with William Pars, an artist noted for his topographical drawings of Irish and continental scenes, some of which were engraved, and who at the outset of his career also painted miniatures. In 1775 he was given a small pension of £60 from the Dillettanti Society with which to study art in Italy, and he left for Rome in October of that year, apparently accompanied by Mrs Smart. He took with him a letter of introduction to Sir William Mann from Horace Walpole dated 23 October 1775. A further letter from Walpole to Mann on 14 November stated that Pars was detained in Paris, having lost his portmanteau between Calais and Paris and with it all his possessions.

Thomas Jones mentions in his diary of 27 November 1776 that he met Pars in Rome on his arrival, and there are several references to the three of them meeting on other occasions.

In the *Memoirs of Thomas Jones* (Walpole Society, Vol. XXXII) a full description is given of Mrs Pars' death in Rome and the events which led up to it:

This lady was in fact wife to Smart the Miniature painter, and a most fatal Connexion it was for my poor friend as will appear by what follows— When Pars return'd from Asia-Minor, whither he had been sent as Draftsman by the Dilletante Society in company with Messr. Revett & Chandler— among other old acquaintances, used to visit Smart—Everybody who knew Smart must know, however eminent he was in his profession, that he was a man of the most vulgar manners, grossly sensual, and greedy of Money to an extreme—(I have often heard him say 'D—— me Sir I can Sit on my A—— for 18 hours together without stirring & put four & twenty guineas in my pocket at a Sitting').

His wife was a high spirited, handsome Girl whom he had picked up at one of the Bagnios about Covent Garden—She had a taste for Poetry and elegant Amusements—He was a Muckworm—And as his brutal appetites were sufficiently satiated, he treated her with rude neglect—Nobody scarcely but Smart could have thought of engaging Pars as Cavalier servantes to his wife—a thoughtless gay young fellow of an Amorous Constitution—but this very character, induced the Other to fix upon him to attend Mrs S at her Country lodgings while he was busy at home, making his fortune—Is it to be wondered at, that under such circumstances, an attachment should have taken place?—The consequence was, that Smart separated from his Wife; and Pars, like another Mark Antony, neglected all other pursuits for her—with such an inattention to Business, finding he could not remain long in England, and being naturally of a roving disposition—He accepted of, from the same Society, a small pension of 60 pounds a Year to study in Italy 3 Years—With this scanty allowance and a few Commissions from a Nobleman of Taste (L—d Palmerston) with whom he had, at a former time, made the tour of Ireland, he set off with the Lady, and after being robd of his Trunk and little All, which was cut from behind the chaise as he was passing a wood in France and waiting in Paris 'till he had received a fresh supply from the above Nobleman—he arrived at Rome a few months before me—Pars was well aware that Smart waited only for Sufficient Evidence to substantiate a criminal process against him—That was his Intention and for that purpose cultivated my Acquaintance as much as he could before I set off for Italy—and after I had arrived at Rome, kept teazing me with Letters on the Subject—but as I despised the idea of being employ'd as a Spy on my friend's transactions—I only answered 'That there was a Lady who went by such a name, but as I never had seen her before I saw her at Rome, I could not pretend to ascertain who She really was—and that as She was then in a deep Consumption, and in all probability would be no more by the time he received my Letter—it was of very little Consequence'—the Lady dyed, as I had foretold a few Days afterward—which relieved Pars from the Embarrassment, and myself from Smart's Correspondence.[1]

Unfortunately none of the letters referred to from Smart has been preserved, but as Jones himself was living with his landlady's daughter in 1779, by whom he had two illegitimate daughters, and Pars was boarding with him at the time, it would appear that they were in no position to censure others.

A further reference to Mrs Pars' death and funeral is to be found in *Memorials of an Eighteenth Century Painter, James Northcote*, edited by Stephen Gwyn.

I attended one funeral in Rome—that of an Englishwoman, the wife of Pars an English Painter, who died there. The company, all English, who attended this ceremony, went in hired coaches, about eleven o'clock at night, as private and as quick as possible to avoid the impertinence of the

[1] Walpole Society, Vol. XXXII, pp. 73 and 74.

Common people. Mr Pars went himself in that coach which contained the corps of his late wife in her coffin, the rest of the company in two other coaches. The burying ground is in a field outside the walls of the city, where the Protestants of all nations are permitted to bury their dead.

As the company arrived at the burial-place with great expedition, they had but few followers, and those few behaved with much decorum.

The husband of the deceased gave gloves to all his friends who attended the funeral according to the English custom, also a large wax torch to each, to light at the place of interment, which was at the base of the pyramid, the tomb of the ancient Roman, Caius Cestus.

There being no Protestant priest at the time in Rome, Mr Banks, the Sculptor, read the funeral service. The whole ceremony had an awful though forlorn and dreary effect, and strongly pressed on all present the feeling of being in a foreign land. The service being ended, they extinguished their torches, and returned to their homes in peace.

No record can be found of this burial, which is not surprising under the circumstances and in view of the fact that few records were kept at that time, and if they were, have most probably since been destroyed.[1]

After his first wife left him, Smart formed a connexion with a lady called Sarah Midgeley, by whom he had a son, John Smart, Junior (1776–1809) and a daughter, Sarah (1781–1853). Evidence for this attachment is to be found in the Guardianship Proceedings of the Court of Chancery for 1790, where there are references to arrangements relating to the care, maintenance, and education of these infants, as well as adequate provision for their mother; for on 26 March 1785, before he sailed for India, Smart signed a document appointing Thomas Parkinson and Philip Paumier as guardians of the children and formed a trust for their benefit and that of their mother. Smart must have kept in close touch with their affairs and was evidently far from satisfied with the way in which his trust was being carried out, nor did he like the school selected for Sarah, that of Mrs Cresswell of Boston Road, Brentford. Consequently on 14 October 1788 he executed a Deed-Poll at Fort St George, appointing Edmund Monk, of Fleet Street, London (a jeweller), and Robert Bowyer (Smart's former pupil and miniature painter to the Royal Family), jointly to be his attorneys, to manage his estate and supervise the education of his two children. A number of letters dealing with the matter, written by Smart to Bowyer, were produced to the Court on 13 February 1790, with the result that Robert Bowyer was given the guardianship of the children, the Master, Edward Montague, being satisfied that he was a fit and proper person to fulfil this office.

Before he left England, Smart had arranged with his trustees that

[1] Gwynn, *Memorials of an Eighteenth Century Painter*, London, 1898, pp. 158–60.

certain leasehold property in Water Lane, Fleet Street, should be kept for the use of Sarah Midgeley and the children. From this it is clear that Smart did all in his power to make provision for the children and to safeguard their interests, and, as will be seen in subsequent chapters, was concerned for their welfare throughout his life. It is quite evident that Thomas Jones's assessment of his character was very one-sided.

CHAPTER TWO

Life in India

IN VIEW of the stories of vast sums of money to be made in India, it was not surprising that Smart decided to follow the lead set by many others, though, like them, he was to discover that fortunes were not so readily made. Commissions from Indian princes were easy enough to obtain, but the exalted sitters were notoriously bad payers. Consequently patronage came from employees of the East India Company; but although in the early days they were comparatively rich, this state of affairs did not last and incomes gradually declined, with the result that artists were employed less and many returned to England, disappointed at having failed to obtain the vast fortune they had expected.

On 28 July 1784, Smart was granted permission to leave England for India and take with him his daughter, Anna Maria, who was then 18 years old.

In the records of the East India Company *Public Sundries*, 1787-8, Vols. 40-41, page 170, is a copy of a letter:

Sir,

The order of the Company of April 1777 requiring everyone to give their names who do not belong to the Company and the means by which they come to India really totally slipt my memory. I therefore now inform you I had the Court of Directors full assent to come out to follow my profession of painting and to bring my daughter with me. I sail'd April the 19th, 1785, from England on Board the Dutton, Capt. West ; and arrived at Madras the 6th of Septr. following in the same vessell.

I am,
Sir,
Your most obdt. servt.
JOHN SMART.

Madras,
19th Decr. 1787.

In a list in the *Public Dispatches from England*, 1784–5, Vol. 88, the name of John Smart, miniature painter, and Anna Maria Smart appear among the list of passengers on board the *Dutton*, which sailed from England on 19 April 1785 bound for Madras, their destination being given as Fort St George. The ship arrived at Madras on 6 September 1785, and the Smarts took up residence in North Street, sometimes known as Middlegate Street, Fort St George.

In a letter dated 9 December 1784, the Court of Directors informed the necessary authority that:

> Mr John Smart, Miniature Painter and Messrs Ozias Humphry and Francis Wheatley, Portrait Painters have obtained our permission to proceed to East Indies to follow their profession there.[1]

Many other portrait painters and miniaturists were in India about this time, including Zoffany, Tilly Kettle, John Aldfounder, Samuel Andrews, Thomas Daniell, R.A., William Daniell, R.A., T. Hickey, R.A., Mrs Diana Hill, William Hodges, R.A., and Charles Shirreff.

The artist most perturbed by Smart's desire to go to India was Ozias Humphry (1742–1810), who feared the competition might seriously affect his position. Writing to his brother, he says he had learned with infinite regret that three other artists had decided to go out to India, amongst whom 'is Mr Smart which I am particularly concerned to hear, as it will very much militate with my views, as will my being there with his'. Later he says that the news of Smart's determination to go to India was 'great mortification' to him, but made him all the more anxious to set out. Humphry was well aware of Smart's ability and was most anxious that he should get established in India before the latter arrived, for he also knew that his work, though good, was inferior to Smart's.[2] Humphry was anxious to be one of the first artists to go to India, and said he hoped his having gone out would 'discourage others from quitting England'. He instructed his brother to keep his intentions 'a profound secret', or if he did mention it to put people off the scent, as it was 'most important that he should be in India before John Smart'.

Before leaving England, Humphry had been paying attention to Miss Mary Boydell, whose uncle, John Boydell, an engraver and print publisher, was an important person in London, serving in turn the offices of Alderman, Sheriff, and in 1790 Lord Mayor. Boydell had no family, but had adopted and brought up his two nieces; Humphry had every reason

---

[1] *Public Dispatches*, 1784–8, Vol. 88, p. 13.
[2] Williamson, *Ozias Humphry*, pp. 118 and 119.

to think these girls would inherit considerable fortunes and envisaged himself married to Mary, thus reaping the benefit. The uncle, however, was not in favour of this attachment and disliked any correspondence between the two. Humphrey did not commit himself to an engagement before going to India and appears to have thought that the lady was his for the asking.

After arriving in India, Humphry learnt that both the Alderman and his niece were having their miniatures painted by Smart, and in a letter to Miss Boydell he says that if Smart is not able to paint her portrait because of his intended departure for India he hopes she will employ Jeremiah Meyer or any painter other than Cosway (Cosway's reputation as a flirt being well known). Humphry then tells her that he would much prefer Smart to paint her, because it was sure to be a good portrait and worthy of her, and hopes that she will urge him to carry out the commission. He then goes further and suggests that she might encourage all her friends to sit to Smart, so that he might think it worth deferring his trip to India until the next winter.

In due course Humphry received from Miss Boydell a case containing the portrait of herself by Smart, and one of her uncle by one of Smart's pupils. Humphry pronounced the portrait of Miss Boydell to be an excellent likeness, but without any flattery, 'and imagines that its unsatisfactory appearance to him has been very largely due to the state of her health'.[1]

Later, when Humphry decided to go to Delhi and Agra, he wrote to Miss Boydell that he 'regretted leaving Calcutta because it may then make room for Mr Smart who is now at Madras'[2]—adding that if Smart came to Calcutta he might have to take up painting in oil in order to compete with him, the only oil painters there being Thomas Hickey and Zoffany, who was on the point of returning to England.

After exchanging letters for some time, Miss Boydell wrote to Humphry on 15 November 1786 that she no longer wished to continue their friendship, and was returning to his brother various items including a miniature of himself, and requested that he should return the case containing her portrait and all her letters.

As things turned out Humphry need not have bothered himself so much about his rival, for Smart, in spite of rumours to the contrary, remained in Madras for practically the whole of his time in India. He was much employed as miniature painter to Muhammad Ali, the Nawab

[1] Williamson, *Ozias Humphry*, pp. 128 and 129.
[2] Williamson, *Ozias Humphry*, pp. 128 and 129.

of Arcot, and his family and his services were in great demand by Government officials, the officers of the Army, and other English residents. Unfortunately he did not receive all the money due to him from the Nawab and was still owed 4,114 pagodas when he left the country.

A brief description of Madras is given in *The Indian Empire*, by R. Montgomery Martin, and is as follows:

> Madras on the Coromandel Coast, consists of three broad streets, running North and South, dividing the town into four nearly equal parts. They are well built, and contain the principle European shops. On the beach is a line of Public Offices including the Supreme Court, the Customs House, the Marine Board Office and the offices and storehouses of the Principle European Merchants. The other buildings are, the Mint, the Roman Catholic Cathedral, the Church Mission Chapel, Armenian Church, Trinity Chapel, the General Hospital and Medical School. Fort St George is in form an irregular polygon somewhat of a semi-circle of which the sea face which is well armed with heavy guns, is nearly a diameter. No part is probably more than twenty feet above the sea level.[1]

Basil Long refers to two undated newspapers, but probably of 1788, preserved at the Victoria and Albert Museum which report: 'Mr Smart is in such deserved estimation in the East Indies that no other miniature painter can meet encouragement; he is still at Madras, but his presence at Calcutta and Lucknow is so earnestly courted that none of the Chiefs will submit to be painted by any other artist.' Another newspaper dated 1789 states: 'Smart, the predecessor of Bowyer, has painted everybody at Bombay, and is gone to Bengal.'[2]

Some months after their arrival in Madras, Anna Maria was married on 11 July 1786 to Robert Woolf of the Madras Civil Service, by whom she had nine children, Robert, Anna Sophia, Elizabeth Anne, Anna Carolina, Maria, John William (born at St Helena), William Henry, George Balfour, and Charlotte Emma. After this marriage, Smart's other daughter, Sophia, was, according to the Court Minutes of 3 December 1788, granted permission to go to India and join her father. This she did, and before long became engaged, and on 8 February 1790 married Lieutenant (afterwards Lieutenant-General) John Dighton (1761–1840). She did not survive the birth of their son John, whose baptism, together with that of his cousin, Maria Woolf, is recorded as taking place on 20 May 1794.

Also living in Madras was Lieutenant-Colonel Charles Smart, who

[1] R. Montgomery Martin, *The Indian Empire*, 1861, Vol. III, p. 70.
[2] Basil Long, *The British Miniaturist*, London, 1929.

appears from records in the possession of the Grindon family to have been either a brother or cousin to John Smart.[1] He was married at Madras on 4 September 1792 to Sarah Ann, daughter of John Barlow and his wife, Sarah, who was a sister to Robert Woolf. Sarah Ann and Charles had one son, Hamilton Edmund. In Sarah Ann Smart's will, after bequests to her servants, she left her estate divided into four equal parts, the legatees being her son Hamilton, her father, her aunt Elizabeth Woolf, and her cousin Robert Woolf of the 6th Native Cavalry. After her father's death she made a codicil, dated 30 June 1819, by which she revoked the share to her aunt, leaving her estate divided equally between her son and her cousin.[2] Mrs Woolf is thought to have taken some part in supervising the welfare of Anna Maria's children whilst the parents were in India, and may well have also looked after Charles Kenworthy, the natural son of Colonel Smart, born five years before his marriage.

Charles Kenworthy Smart, the name of whose mother is unknown, was born on 29 May 1787, and baptized at St Mary's Church, Fort St George. He was educated in London and a portrait of him was at one time in the possession of Sophia Grindon, and later of Mrs Mabel G. Hughes, both descendants of John Smart. In 1803, Charles became a cadet, and was commissioned a lieutenant in 1804, sailing to India on the *Lord Nelson* on 18 February of that year, to join the 1st Madras Infantry Regiment. He was killed in a mutiny at Vellore on 10 July 1806, at the hands of his own soldiers, who betrayed his hiding-place and that of two brother officers.

This incident was a regrettable one, brought about by the enforcement of certain regulations in dress contrary to the manners and customs of the native troops, and enforced without the knowledge of Lord William Bentinck, who succeeded Lord Clive in the Government of Madras. The new regulations required the sepoys to appear on parade with their chins clean shaved and the hair shaved off their upper lip. They were not to wear the distinguishing marks of their cast, or wear ear-rings when in uniform, but were to wear a turban of a new pattern. This caused great feeling among the troops, who thought that the turban they were required to wear was devised in order to convert them to Christianity. Two of Tippo Sahib's sons, who were State prisoners at Vellore and had been allowed considerable freedom and a princely income during their captivity, took this opportunity to incite the troops to mutiny. No notice was taken of the growing rumours of disaffection, and on 10 July 1806

[1] Descendants of Smart, see Family Tree.
[2] Commonwealth Relations Office.

the European part of the garrison at Vellore was attacked by their native soldiers. In consequence of this mutiny and massacre of the English garrison which the prisoners had encouraged, they were removed to Fort St George, and from there to Fort William in Bengal.

Two drawings by Smart of particular interest are those of the sons of Tippo Sahib now preserved at the British Museum. The portraits are of Abdul Khalick, the eldest, and Mooiz ud Din, the third son, and are both dated 1794. In *Travels in India*,[1] Thomas Twining says that he visited them on 8 August 1792. He was introduced to the two young princes by Colonel Doveton of the Madras Army, and gives the following description of the meeting:

> . . . on our entering their rooms they seemed quite glad to see us, asked us through Colonel Doveton, inquired whether we had breakfasted, our names, and many other questions. There is not much difference in their size. The youngest, named Mirza, is most pleasing. He is fair, with large, handsome eyes. He was very cheerful and polite; talked a great deal to us, and very sensibly, though not eight years of age. When he heard that we should see Lord Cornwallis, he desired, with tears in his eyes, to be remembered to him. 'Tell Lord Cornwallis that he is always with me.'

Twining goes on to say:

> Mr Smart, a miniature painter, who told me to my surprise that he had taken my mother's picture, was taking their likenesses. They are to be sent when finished to Tippo Sahib; for Lord Cornwallis having asked him if he would like to have his sons' pictures, 'Yes,' said he, 'provided they be accompanied by Lord Cornwallis's.'

The boys were apparently well provided for with servants and had a handsome stage built for them in order that they might see the ships.

Whether Tippo Sahib ever saw the drawings we do not know, but they are interesting reminders of the incident. If any miniatures existed, their whereabouts are unknown.

Details on the back of the drawings are:

1st boy eldest son of Tippo
2nd boy third son of Tippo
Delivered up to Marquis Cornwallis in the camp before Seringapatam Feb. 14 1792. Remarkably fair regular features and small round face and animated appearance.
Drawings executed soon after his arrival at Madras.[2]

Other interesting reminders of this association are a medal, with

[1] Twining, *Travels in India*, p. 66.
[2] Modern spelling of Tippo or Tippoo is Tipu.

Cornwallis's bust on the obverse, and Tippo Sahib handing the two boys over to Cornwallis on the reverse, and a coloured mezzotint depicting the scene.

Lord Cornwallis took over the post of Governor-General and Commander-in-Chief in India and Calcutta in 1786 and, after a distinguished career, was created Marquis Cornwallis in 1792. A miniature of him by Smart, signed and dated 1787, is now at the Fitzwilliam Museum, Cambridge. Other miniatures by Smart, dated 1793, of both the Marquis and Lady Cornwallis, were exhibited at 158b New Bond Street, London, in 1911, and a superb sketch dated 1792 was in Sir Bruce Ingram's collection.

Many preliminary sketches for miniatures made by Smart in India have been preserved, as have a number of those drawn on board the *Dutton* and the *Melville Castle* on his passages out and home. Some of them, notably those of Baker, quartermaster of the *Dutton*, in Miss Felicity Jaffé's collection, and of Captain Hayes of the *Melville Castle*, in my own collection, are distinctly amusing.

Smart had a distinguished patronage throughout the whole of his time in India. Among his sitters were Sir Charles and Lady Oakeley (Sir Charles was Governor of Madras in 1790 and was responsible for some fine administration in connexion with the finance of the area); Sir Archibald Campbell (1739–91), Governor of Madras from 1786 to 1789, and Lady Campbell; Sir William Cockburn (1768–1835), who served as a lieutenant-colonel in India from 1790 to 1802; Sir John MacPherson (1745–1821), whose miniature Smart painted on 16 October 1787, a writer under the East India Company at Madras 1770–6; Colonel Henry Watson, painted before 1786; Henry Crawford; General Sir Robert Sloper, K.B., member of Council at Fort William, painted in 1787; Josias Dupré Porcher; Thomas Chase; Sir Alexander Allan, whose miniature is in the Fitzwilliam Museum; Sir Samuel Young; James Charles Stuart Strange; Thomas Cockburn, M.C.S.; James Dighton; Captain Speedway; Benjamin Roebuck; Sir John Floyd; General Colin Macaulay (now at Kings College, Cambridge); Muhammud Ali Khan of whom several miniatures are known to exist; John Constantine Phipps; Dr James Anderson, botanist, Physician General and President of the Medical Board at Madras.

Of Smart's life and habits in India we know nothing. The often-quoted reference to Miss Dalling having met Smart and his son in India must be inaccurate, in view of the fact that they were not in the country together. There is no doubt that had Smart remained longer in Madras he would not have lacked patrons, and despite the difficulty he experienced in obtaining the payments due to him from the Nawab of Arcot and others, he must have succeeded in making quite a considerable sum of money without having to travel to other parts of India, which was the fate of most other artists who went out to 'shake the pagoda tree'.

CHAPTER THREE

Return to London

JOHN SMART returned to London in the winter of 1795 after passing ten very successful years in India. He left Madras on 27 April, on the *Melville Castle*, which arrived at St Helena on 15 August. There he joined his daughter Anna Maria Woolf and her family, who accompanied him for the rest of the voyage. On 20 October of the previous year Mrs Woolf and four of her chidren, Anna Sophia, Elizabeth Anne, Anna Carolina, and Maria, together with her nephew, John Dighton, and two maids, a black girl called Matilda, and Rebecca Jones with her infant son of nine months, set sail for England on the *Dutton*. They reached St Helena on 9 January 1795, and the family were obliged to disembark to enable Mrs Woolf to give birth to her sixth child, John William.

The *Melville Castle* left St Helena on 5 September and the passengers went ashore at Portsmouth on 19 November. Smart then took up residence at 20 Grafton Street, London, moving later to 2 Russell Place, Fitzroy Square,[1] and it was to this house that he took his second wife, Edith (Vere?) in about 1799. Records of this marriage have been searched for in vain. The only authority to give the name of Vere was Dr G. C. Williamson, but the source of his information cannot be traced.[2] We do know, however, that Smart presented Edith with a profile silhouette, said to be of himself, painted on ivory and executed by an unknown artist about 1800. The frame, made of gold, was decorated with blue and white enamel and engraved on the back in the following way:

Edith
from her husband
John Smarte
Russell Place
Fitzroy Sq.

[1] Renamed Fitzroy Street in 1866.
[2] Williamson, *Portrait Miniatures*, London, 1897, p. 49.

This profile does not bear a close resemblance to the artist and may well have been of some other member of the family. It was formerly in the late Francis and Minnie Wellesley's collection, and was on loan to the Victoria and Albert Museum in 1913, when it was described as the only existing portrait of John Smart. It is now in the collection of Mrs Burton Jones,[1] who possesses one of the finest collections of Smart's work in Britain.

Neither the exact date of this marriage nor that of Edith's death are known, but both events must have taken place between his return to London in 1795 and 14 February 1805, when he described himself as a widower at the time of his marriage to his third wife, Mary Morton.[2]

The England to which Smart had returned was not a peaceful one. Arthur Byrant describes the years from 1793 to 1802 as *The Years of Endurance*, which indeed they were for many people. Threat of a Napoleonic invasion hung over the country, and it was necessary to raise more units of volunteers, of which 40,000 were enrolled in London alone. Smart was among those who enlisted, and in the MSS. of *Farington Diary* at Windsor there are several entries relating to the part played by him and Robert Smirke, together with other artists, in forming the St Pancras Volunteers in 1798.[3] Robert Smirke and Samuel Foote, both friends of his, lived in the vicinity of Fitzroy Square. In 1796 Smirke exhibited a picture entitled *The Conquest* at the Royal Academy; Mr Jaffé contended that the person posing in the picture was in all probability Smart and that the fur-trimmed coat worn by the sitter was like that worn by Smart in the portrait painted of him by Richard Brompton in about 1780.[4]

The Incorporated Society of Artists, with which he had been so closely connected, had ceased to exist by the time he returned to England, and the belief that he lost a considerable sum of money when it was wound up cannot be verified. No doubt many patrons were eagerly awaiting his return and he was soon in as great demand in London as he had been in India.

The only banking account that can be traced is the one he opened at Coutts on 26 April 1802. There was never any substantial sum of money in this account for long, and he borrowed between £100 and £160 each year in January or February, repaying it the following month after the

[1] Jaffé, *The Art Quarterly*, 1954, p. 245.
[2] Marriage Register, St Marylebone Church.
[3] *Farington Diary*, Windsor Typescript, 1798.
[4] Now in the collection of Mr and Mrs J. Starr, Kansas City.

receipt of money from interests in India. This temporary embarrassment may have been due to the failure of some of his clients to pay for their commissions, or this may have been a special account mainly for the purpose of receiving money from India. The Nawab of Arcot's debt had not been settled, and on 15 May 1804 interest was claimed on this amount at 6 per cent from 6 September 1795 to the above date, making a total of 6,260.34.66 pagodas or £2,504. 6s. 7d. at 8s. per pagoda. From his will, we know that he was owed money by others in Madras and London, and that he had investments in the East Indies. The only record we have of Smart's income from painting is to be found in *Farington Diary* for 28 July 1798: 'Smart says he has realized between 5 & £600 a year. He paints miniatures now at 25 guineas a head.'[1]

As has already been mentioned, Smart married for the third and last time on 14 February 1805, at St Marylebone Church, London, his bride being Mary Morton; they had one son, John James. Farington records that Mary 'seems to be a well disposed woman & Has brought Him to habits of regularity in attending Divine Service'.[2] Several portraits of her exist, the two earliest being identical sketches drawn before their marriage. On one is pencilled 'Sept 1804', when Smart also noted that she was 21 on 14 February 1804. This portrait formerly belonged to Mrs Dyer, one of her great-grandchildren. Another miniature of Mary, painted in 1809, was formerly in the collection of another great-grandchild, Mrs Busteed, on the reverse of which was a lock of hair and a monogram. Mary Morton was a member of the Church of England, and on the flyleaf of her Prayer Book, which was published by the Clarendon Press in 1799, is written:

> *Mary Morton*
> *Sept. 5 1801*
> *ever pray for me.*

and in what appears to be her husband's handwriting is an entry relating to the birth of their son John James as follows:

> *John James Smart*
> *born the 7th of October 1805 at twenty*
> *minutes before two in the afternoon*
> *a very fine sunshine afternoon.*

On the next page is another entry, which refers to the birth of a daughter to John James and his wife Elizabeth, *née* Bailey.

[1] *Farington Diary*, Windsor Typescript.
[2] *Farington Diary*, Greig Edit., Vol. VI, p. 10.

Mary Ann Smart
Born 9th of June 1856
at half past nine in the morning
A very fine morning.

This Prayer Book, now the property of Mr J. W. Busteed, was formerly in the possession of Mrs Dyer, who also had, among other things, one of John Smart's paint brushes, which had been given to her by her grandmother, Elizabeth Smart. The Prayer Book and other relics were sent to me recently by Mr Busteed and have provided valuable information.

From at least 1806 Smart gave money to his daughter Sarah, who had continued to live at Russell Place, and on 21 June 1808 an indenture was drawn up settling a considerable sum of money on her.[1]

His sister, Deborah Wright, received small sums of money from time to time[2] and provision was also made for her under his will. Mrs Wright made her will as a widow on 20 November 1818, leaving her estate to her daughter, Lydia, wife of James Eagle or Eagles. She died on 10 May 1822, and her daughter and the other executors—William Downes and William Cole—administered her estate, which amounted to only £450.

Smart painted in 1806 a very fine miniature of a young actor whose name is now almost forgotten, but who at the time made a great impression on all who enjoyed the theatre. This was William Henry West Betty, or the Young Roscius, as he was called. At the age of 9 the boy had been taken to see Mrs Siddons act and was so inspired that he insisted on becoming an actor. When he was 11 years of age he made his first appearance on the stage at Belfast, where he was engaged for four nights, and on the last one played Romeo to a delighted audience. In 1803 he played Hamlet in Dublin and from there went to Cork, Waterford, and in the following spring to Glasgow and Edinburgh. A year later he appeared at Covent Garden and Drury Lane and was received with such enthusiasm that on one occasion the police had to be called in to keep order. So great was his success that Pitt is said to have adjourned the House of Commons in order that its members could be in time to see him play. His last appearance as a boy actor was at Bath in 1808. Smart painted his portrait in 1806 and Farington refers to this fact in his *Diary* on 11 May 1806, when he says: 'We also met Smart who had been walking to Hampstead. He shewed us a miniature picture of Master Betty, which He had just finished. It was like the Boy—Smart was, as usual, very much

[1] See Chapter Five.
[2] Messrs Coutts & Co.

delighted with his own performance.'[1] This miniature was exhibited at the Royal Academy in 1808. Curiously enough, it is the only item relating to sitters that can be traced in Smart's accounts. It was paid for on 5 September 1806, the sum being £39. 12s. 6d.

In May 1808, Smart wrote to the Court of Directors of the East India Company, asking permission for his son, John Smart, Junior, to go to India and practise as a miniature painter.[2] The young man had been living with his father at Russell Place and was already known as a miniaturist. Having obtained the necessary permission, he left England in August 1808, but died in the following June before he had been long in India. The news of his death must have come as a great shock to his father and must have been totally unexpected, or the young man would never have left this country. On 4 August 1809 Farington met Smart, who told him that he had not been well and that he had been suffering from uneasiness of mind. This was no doubt partly due to his son's death. Smart said that his own health was improving and that he had been advised to go to the seaside.[3]

Two years later Smart made his will. It was carefully thought out, and in great detail, making adequate provision for his wife and young son, John James, as well as bequeathing an annuity of £60 to his sister, Deborah Wright, £30 to 'Millercent Hitchings', a maid, and ten guineas to each of his Trustees, to purchase a ring in his memory. After payment of his bequests, the life interest on his estate went to his wife. His son John James received £1,000 on attaining the age of twenty-one and the residue of the estate on the death of his mother. In the event of his son not surviving, and having no issue, the £1,000 was to go to his daughter, Anna Maria Woolf, in trust for her daughter Sophia, the residue of the estate to be divided between all surviving children of Mrs Woolf. As this contingency did not arise, the Woolf family derived no benefit from his will.

On 22 March 1811, only a month before he died, he withdrew all remaining sums from Coutts and closed his account. This was reopened by his executors on 24 June 1811 and not finally closed until 4 November 1834. The inventory made of his effects on 13 May 1811 and signed by Thomas Tims of 57 Upper Charlotte Street, Fitzroy Square, and Mr Perkins, No. 12 Little Charlotte Street, Goodge Street, and the executors, William Ruddiman, Mary Smart, and Joseph Nollekens, gives an idea

---

[1] *Farington Diary*, Greig Edit., Vol. III, p. 226.
[2] Chapter Six.
[3] *Farington Diary*, Greig Edit., Vol. V, p. 217.

of the house, which had eight main rooms and kitchen premises. The contents were valued at £145. 12*s*., and Mary Smart agreed to retain these for her use on condition that she should deliver them over to the trustees on request or repay them the sum of £145. 12*s*.

It is interesting to note that in J. T. Smith's description of Joseph Nollekens' sitting-room mention is made of three miniatures which hung over the chimney-piece; one was of Sir Joshua Reynolds, by Edridge, and the other two, by Smart, were of Mrs Nollekens and Miss Welch, her sister. All of them, says Mr Smith, 'were presented by the artists'.

The date of Mary Smart's marriage to John Sidey Caley has not been found, and although she is still referred to in Coutt's ledgers as Mrs Smart up to July 1812, in a copy of the executors' accounts dated 27 September 1811 there is an entry recording her payment of £69. 10*s*. to the executors for the part payment of the household effects left by John Smart. She is described here as 'Mrs Smart, now Caley'.

In 1813 there was a balance of £77. 0*s*. 11*d*., and the executors agreed to pay Mrs Caley £20 per month from 15 October for the maintenance of herself and John James until the balance was used up. The executors wrote to Messrs Coutts on 1 December 1814 requesting them to pay Mrs Wright her half-yearly payment of £30 and to honour Mrs Caley's draft countersigned by her husband, John Sidey Caley. A memorandum was signed on 24 November 1814 relating to the legacy for John James which gives the amount of John Smart's estate as £8,942. 18*s*. 3*d*. It reads as follows:

1814 November 24th.

Memorandum in the above mentioned sums of £8,845.13.10 and £97.4.5 £4 p.c. Consolidated Bank Annuities standing in one Name in the Books of the Governor and Company of the Bank of England as Trustees and Executors under the will of the said John Smart is included a legacy of one thousand pounds bequeathed by the Testator to his son John James Smart as Stated in the foregoing Account and the same Legacy of £1,000 is fully understood and admitted to form part of the said p.c. Bank Annuities and is so arranged in consequence of no special appropriation having occurred or been made for the purpose of its distinct investment—signed

JOSEPH NOLLEKENS
WILLIAM RUDDIMAN
MARY CALEY

Signed by the said
Joseph Nollekens
William Ruddiman and
Mary Caley in the
presence of John Tims.

The assessment of Smart's character given by Thomas Jones is not sustained by the facts that have since been discovered. From his will, and the Chancery Court proceedings relating to his mistress and two illegitimate children, the provision for Sarah and his sister, Deborah, it is quite clear that Smart was a good businessman and that he took care to make arrangements for anyone dependent on him, or for whom he had any regard. His will was, as far as we know, his last business transaction of any importance, for it will be remembered that he had already closed his account at Coutts the month before.

He died on 1 May 1811, and in the *Gentleman's Magazine* there is this obituary: 'In his 70th year, after an illness of only nine days, John Smart, Esq., of Russell Place, Fitzroy Square, miniature painter. To most philanthropic and hospitable principles, he added great eminence as an artist; his surprising likenesses in miniature being justly admired both in his native country and the East Indies, where he practised for some years with great and deserved reputation.'[1] He was buried in the St James's Burial Ground, Hampstead Road, St Pancras, Middlesex. St James's Church no longer exists and the disused burial ground is now called St James's Gardens. The tombstones which are scattered around the edge of the garden are so weathered as to be indistinguishable.

The inscription which the family placed upon his monument is recorded in Cansick's *Monumental Inscriptions*, and is as follows:

In Memory of
John Smart Esqre
of Russell Place Fitzroy Square
Who departed this life
May 1st 1811 aged
69 years
Deeply lamented by his family and numerous Friends.

Oh Smart in thy works the world will ever see
How great the loss of Art in losing thee
But love and sorrow find their works too weak
Natures keen suffering on thy death to speak
Through all her duties what a heart was thine
In this cold dust what spirit used to shine
Fancy and truth and gaiety and zeal
What most we love in life and losing feel
Age after age may not one artist yield
Equal to thee in painting nicer fields
And ne'er shall sorrowing earth to heaven commend
A fonder parent or a truer Friend.

[1] *Gentleman's Magazine*, 1811, Vol. LXXXI, Part I, p. 599.

CHAPTER FOUR

Smart the Artist

WITHOUT IN any way comparing the work of John Smart with that of any other artist, it cannot be denied that it is of the highest quality, that the draughtsmanship is superb and the colouring exquisite. There is nothing spectacular about the miniatures he painted, nor did he find it necessary for his sitters to be in elaborate clothing. The women were painted in simple dresses, with attractive coiffeurs, and the general effect was soft and harmonious. His portraits of men and of women were equally successful whether the sitters wore plain clothes or uniform, and an examination of his work brings one to the conclusion that he had an unmistakable gift for catching a likeness, and that the finished portraits undoubtedly represented the sitters with truth and accuracy.

In 1921 Dr G. C. Williamson asserted that 'the noblest and most dignified miniatures of the eighteenth century were undoubtedly those painted by John Smart', not that they are the most fascinating portraits of the period, 'but when properly understood and appreciated, they will be found to be worthy of greater study'.[1] Basil Long, writing of Smart eight years later, says, 'he is one of the greatest miniaturists of the English School',[2] and Graham Reynolds, writing in 1952, says that Smart's miniatures 'are esteemed by many collectors as ardently as those of Richard Cosway, and some even seek to give him higher place'.[3] In an article in 1936 in the *Bazaar Exchange and Mart* he is described as the 'greatest English Miniaturist of the Eighteenth Century', and the author notes that his work is 'not perhaps so widely appreciated as its merits warrant'. The article goes on to point out that 'although every novice collector of miniatures is determined to own a Cosway, few know much

[1] Williamson, *The Miniature Collector*, p. 131.
[2] Long, *British Miniaturists*, 1929.
[3] Reynolds, *English Portrait Miniatures*, 1953, p. 151.

about Smart'. This could hardly be said to be true today, for with a revival of interest in this field of collecting and the fact that a large number of miniatures and sketches have come into the sale-rooms in recent years and fetched high prices, Smart's name has been well publicized, and his portraits have become in great demand. It is interesting to recall that although for many years Smart's miniatures did not obtain these prices, yet in the sale of the late Mr Pierpoint Morgan's collection in 1935 the pair of miniatures of Sir Charles and Lady Oakeley, both signed and dated 1786, made 1,120 guineas the pair. Sir Charles, who was the first baronet, had married in October 1777, Helena, only daughter of Robert Beatson, of Kilrie, Fife, who was for a time Governor of St Helena, hence her Christian name. That the miniatures of Sir Charles and Lady Oakeley fetched such an exceedingly high price was due in part to the fact that three members of the Beatson family were unknowingly bidding against each other! This resulted in the miniatures going into the collection of Lord Bearstead. I am indebted to Madam Stuart Stevenson, one of the three concerned, for this information. These portraits are probably two of the finest examples of Smart's work. A sketch for the one of Lady Oakeley belongs to Mr Peter Jaffé. Lady Oakeley was evidently an accomplished artist, for she copied paintings by well-known artists of members of the family, and Madam Stuart Stevenson presented me with three delightful drawings of family groups drawn in ink and dated February 1771, when Helena Beatson was only 9 years old.

J. J. Foster refers to a miniature which fetched £800 in 1902 and a pair of miniatures of children sold for 240 guineas in 1910.[1]

The superb quality of Smart's draughtsmanship was apparent even in his first drawings when, as a boy of 11, he entered the Society of Arts' (later Royal) first competition in 1755. His subject, a nude male figure posing as a river god, won him second place in the premium awards, as I mentioned in Chapter One. It was an ambitious drawing for a boy of his age for it necessitated a very accurate knowledge of the human figure, as did his drawing of a man startled by a rising serpent, which gained him first prize in 1756, when he was but 12 years old. The following year he drew a portrait in chalk of his drawing master, William Shipley, for which he obtained another premium. His next and last winning drawing at the Society of Arts was of a nude figure of a dancing faun, which he entered in a class for those under 18 years of age, Smart being at that time still only 14 years old. A sketch of a herdsman playing a flute, signed and

[1] Foster, *Dictionary of Painters*, 1926, p. 278.

dated 22 April 1755, was presented to Miss Smirke—a friend of the family—on 22 August 1850. It is now in the collection of Mr Michael Jaffé.

He must have commenced miniature painting almost immediately afterwards, for by 1760 his miniatures were already executed with the perfect draughtsmanship and gemlike brightness that was to be the hallmark of his work throughout his career.

In 1762 he exhibited three items at the Society of Artists—a self-portrait in crayons entitled 'The First Attempt', and two miniatures, one of an unknown man and another of a Jew. These entries were from Dean Street, Soho.

The fact that from the outset he formed the habit of signing and dating his portraits, and adding the Roman I after the date on those painted in India, has helped considerably in placing them in chronological order and in providing a basis of study for those wishing to compare his work with that of his contemporaries. It is also of great value in assessing his merit at all stages of his art. His signature was usually 'J.S.' in cursive initials on the background; the punctuation varies, but the date is almost invariably placed on the line under the initials. Occasionally he signed 'J. Smart' in full, 'J. Smart delin' and a date, 'Jno. Smart delin', and 'John Smart pinxit'. Although a number of his sketches are signed on the reverse and many are not signed at all, he not infrequently made notes about the sitter either on the reverse or round the extreme edge of the portrait near the frame.

The size of his early miniatures was small, about $1\frac{1}{2}$ in., a size which conformed to those ivories used by what Graham Reynolds describes as 'the Modest School of Miniature Painters',[1] those working between 1740 and about 1770. After about 1775, Smart used an ivory of 2 in., increasing to 3 in. in the 1790s and 1800s.

Unlike many other artists, there was not any great change of style or technique in any of his three phases. The portraits are meticulously wrought and drawn in great detail, even in his third and last phase, when he used larger formats. He used a brilliant palate, and his colours have retained their original brightness in a remarkable way, and one rarely, if ever, sees them faded.

His style differed greatly from that of Cosway, whose transparent and light-hearted treatment of his portraits was truly representative of the elegance of the age. Smart, on the other hand, made more extensive use of body colour in the sitters' costumes and used a background that

[1] Reynolds, *English Portrait Miniatures*, 1953.

8
10
9

11

12

PLATE THREE

was inclined to be flat and drab, entirely different from the airy sky backgrounds for which Cosway was so noted. Miniatures by Cosway, Engleheart, and Plimer are all somewhat stylized, with the ladies posing in elaborate dresses and fancy hats, while Smart painted them with an honesty that has an appeal of its own. His aptitude for modelling the features is an unmistakable sign of his work, and the details of the sitters' costumes are painted so dexterously as to make the fabric appear almost as if it could be touched. His flesh colouring tended to be rather a deep red, almost brick red at times, and the highlight of the cheek was accentuated by leaving a small island of naked ivory, whilst a minute spot of opaque white was often placed on the tip of the nose.

One of the things that is unmistakable in Smart's work is the way he painted the lines, and even crow's feet, round the eyes on his sitters' faces, and drew the eyelashes in minute detail, each lash separately. This is particularly apparent in his portraits drawn in profile. From 1760 to about 1766 his shading on the face often had a slightly blue tinge and the draughtsmanship was not so good as that in his miniatures painted after this date, when the use of a blue tint had been abandoned.

Smart's miniatures of children and young people are delightful and give the feeling that the painter was instinctively drawn to the young and understood them. His portraits of women, in addition to being attractive and decorative, have a serenity of expression not always achieved by other painters, and those of men, always meticulously drawn, have a strength of character of their own. With older people he was not, perhaps, quite so successful, but it is always apparent that the portrait is true to life, and that no attempt has been made to glamourize or flatter the sitter.

When drawing hair, whether in its natural state, curled, powdered or partly concealed by a hat or veil, he was always painstaking, and the strands can be discerned without any of the woolliness so often seen in other artists' work. Occasionally he used a pinkish or henna hue in the hair, a habit that in my opinion detracted from the excellence of the painting. Concentration upon the drawing of the features is characteristic of Smart's work; he formed no habit of painting accessories in an attempt to increase the decorative appeal of the picture and details of dress, whether uniform or not, were made entirely subservient to the actual portrait. His one artifice, perhaps, was to draw the features of men, noticeably the eyes and mouth, so as to suggest a sense of humour. This feature is not entirely absent from some of his portraits of women, but the expression is occasionally slightly sardonic.

Backgrounds are, as has been said, restrained and drab, often brown, greenish brown, greenish grey and creamy white. The rarely seen enamel miniatures are almost identical in these respects with those executed in watercolour. It has not been established whether or not Smart ever painted in oil. Basil Long refers to one painted in this medium of Mr Watts of Bengal, but no other examples have so far been traced, and it is possible that the one already mentioned was the work of another artist.

One of his practices was to make sketches on paper, or card, in watercolour or pencil with occasional washes of colour, and of the same size as the finished miniatures. These were usually either of the sitter's head alone, or of head and bust, full length or three-quarter length miniatures being rare. The majority of his sketches were undoubtedly intended as either first drafts or for reference in the event of a duplicate being required. Many of the finest are finished works of art complete in themselves. This is especially true of drawings such as that of Major Robson, Deputy Governor of St Helena, in military uniform, and inscribed:

'John Smart delin: Sept. 1795 St Helena.'

This portrait is now at the British Museum and was bought from the Dyer Sale in 1937. Another example is a miniature of an unknown man, in my collection, in which the face is painted with as much dexterity as would have been a portrait on ivory. Many of the sketches are inscribed with the sitter's name and form a valuable guide to identification.

Three large collections, formerly in the possession of Smart's great-grandchildren, were disposed of between the years 1936 and 1937.[1] On 23 October 1935 one of the owners, Mrs Bose, wife of William Bose, who at one time lived in Edinburgh, took a self-portrait by Smart and a large number of the sketches to the National Gallery of Scotland, whose Director, then Stanley Cursiter, wrote to Basil Long at the Victoria and Albert Museum:

I have just had a visit from Mrs Bose of 2 Darnaway Street, Edinburgh, who brought me a self portrait miniature of John Smart, initialled and dated 1808 I think. This seems to me interesting, but she told me she had dozens more, and this afternoon brought them to me to let me see.

They are evidently Smart's preliminary paintings for his miniatures or possibly copies, which he has done to keep, in many cases they have their names and titles, mostly on paper, with the heads highly finished and the rest of the figure indicated in pencil and evidently cut from a scrap book. There must have been well over a hundred in the bundle I saw and I am told that this is only one third, the remainder being in the possession of sisters-in-law. Her husband is in some way descended from Smart.

[1] See Appendices.

Later in the letter Cursiter continues:

> I should think there is the material here for a memoir on the work of Smart and you are the man to do it.

Unfortunately, within a short time of this letter Basil Long died and the material was dispersed when Mrs Bose[1] and her sisters-in-law, Mrs Dyer and Mrs Busteed, sold their collections. Among the contents of the Busteed sale were interesting studies of hands, dated as late as 1793, and a miniature of Smart's last wife, Mary, dated 1809, which fetched £105. She was painted in a white Empire line dress, wearing a pearl necklace, and the portrait was set in an oval frame, the reverse decorated with a lock of plaited hair and the monogram 'M.S.' In the Dyer collection was the artist's sketch book, containing studies of heads and various drawings of tropical fish, touched with colour. Also in this sale was one of his finest self-portraits painted in 1797—from which year until his death Smart exhibited at the Royal Academy; this portrait now belongs to the Victoria and Albert Museum.

In the same year the artist painted a set of eighteen miniatures of great historic interest; they were of the heroes of the Battle of Camperdown which took place off the Dutch coast on 11 October 1797. These miniatures were engraved by J. Parker and G. Noble with a framework designed by R. Smirke, R.A., and published by R. Bowyer and John Edwards of Pall Mall in 1803.

One of the most interesting collections of portrait miniatures and sketches executed by John Smart is that formerly owned by the late Sir Bruce Ingram. It was unique, for it contained eleven of the eighteen drawings of the heads of these heroes. Smart's drawing of these portraits is, as always, superb; some are executed in pencil only, others have the sitter's coat and any orders in water colour. The portraits are of the following naval officers:

ADMIRAL THE RT HON. VISCOUNT DUNCAN	*Venerable*	74 guns
VICE-ADMIRAL SIR RICHARD ONSLOW, BT	*Monarch*	74 guns
CAPTAIN SIR HENRY TROLLOPE	*Russell*	74 guns
CAPTAIN W. O'BRIEN DRURY	*Powerful*	74 guns
CAPTAIN WILLIAM H. ESSINGTON	*Triumph*	74 guns
CAPTAIN EDWARD O'BRIEN	*Monarch*	64 guns
CAPTAIN JOHN WELLS	*Lancaster*	64 guns

[1] *Jaffé Papers.* Mrs Bose refers to having shown her collection to Basil Long before his death.

CAPTAIN RICHARD R. BURGESS	*Ardent*	64 guns
CAPTAIN WILLIAM BLIGH	*Bounty and Director*	
CAPTAIN JAMES WALKER	*Monmouth*	64 guns
LIEUT. PHILLIPS	*Ardent*	64 guns

The whereabouts of the other sketches is unknown; their subjects were as follows:

CAPTAIN INGLIS	*Belliqueux*	64 guns
CAPTAIN KNIGHT	*Montagu*	74 guns
CAPTAIN SIR W. FAIRFAX	*Venerable*	74 guns
CAPTAIN SIR T. BYARD	*Bedford*	74 guns
CAPTAIN MITCHELL	*Isis*	50 guns
CAPTAIN GREGORY	*Veteran*	64 guns
CAPTAIN HOTHAM	*Adamant*	50 guns

Sir Bruce Ingram also had a superb drawing of the Marquis Cornwallis, signed and dated 1792, Madras, and two other items of interest are the sketch and finished miniature of Captain Pultney Malcolm of the *Donegal*; both are fine examples of Smart's work.

Perhaps the most unusual items are those contained in the artist's sketch book, which was also purchased by Sir Bruce Ingram when the Dyer collection was sold in 1937. This sketch book was undoubtedly that used by Smart on his return voyage from India. It comprises some fifty-six pages of rough sketches, many of them of the coastline of the various places that the ship passed; others are of numerous rather weird-looking heads, and occasionally fishes, dogs, sheep, cows, bears, etc., are also drawn. The most notable pages are those showing the paintings of fish, which, as one would expect, are drawn carefully and in great detail. They are executed in watercolour and pencil and are named as follows: Barnicle, Brown Shark (7 ft long), Leopard Fish, Boncka, Blue Shark (10 ft long), Flying Fish, and the Suckling Fish.

The numerous heads, often as many as twelve or fourteen on a page, may have been of the inhabitants of some of the places *en route*, but the most likely explanation would appear to be that Smart drew them to amuse his grandchildren on the voyage home from St Helena. Many of the heads are slightly alike and drawn at an angle, as if they were sketched in quickly and for fun. One page contains a watercolour sketch of a boat tossed on a stormy sea, and underneath is a recipe for a cure for yellow fever:

On the first symptoms take a small tumbler full of water, strongly impregnated with camomile and magnesia, adding a tablespoon full of citron, Narbonne honey, repeat this 3 or 4 times a day: it will carry away the disorder—that same thing is very good for weak constitutions.

The majority of the sketches of the coastline are unnamed with the exception of the following places: Cape of Good Hope, the Grand Comora, Table Land, Teneriffe, Cape Point, Cape Bona, and Cape Falco. Smart noted the position of the ship on many of the sketches, occasionally giving the distance from the shore. His last sketch is of Gomera, one of the Canary Islands, and after this, in rather faded writing, are the following lines:

A sheppard in clusters crept close by a grove to hide from the heat of the day.

William Bose had evidently made inquiries about the value of Smart's miniatures in 1913, and received a letter from the Reynolds Galleries in London informing him that Smart's miniatures were not then selling quite as well as they did formerly, and that the average price of a male portrait was from £20 to £30 and for a lady, young and good-looking, from £30 to £70.[1]

There is but one record of where Smart bought his materials, a letter from Reeves and Sons in 1953, in which they said that from 1803 to 1808 Smart, then living at 2 Russell Place, bought materials from James Newman of Soho Square, and that he and John Smart, Junior, made the following transactions:

28th April,	1803	£4.	8.	7	
6th May,	1803	8.	18.	–	
6th August,	1803	1.	7.	6	
11th August,	1804		12.	7	
			18.	6	J. Smart, Junior
11th March,	1807		10.	–	
27th August,	1807		18.	–	J. Smart, Junior
22nd February,	1808	3.	12.	–	

Incidentally, Cosway also purchased his materials at Newman's.[2]

In 1785 Smart drew a delightful sketch of the 13-year-old Master John Impey, son of Sir Elijah Impey (later Admiral Impey). This was drawn on board the *Dutton* on the way to Madras. Another striking sketch in profile is that of Major-General Conway, Governor of Pondicherry, drawn in 1792. The same year Smart executed one of the many portraits

[1] *Jaffé Papers.*
[2] *Jaffé Papers.*

he painted of Muhammad Ali, Wallajah, of the Carnatic (1750–95), who appointed him his Court painter and gave him continuous commissions throughout the whole of his time in India, but who omitted to pay the fees and owed a considerable sum of money when the painter left for England.

Another interesting portrait was of Robert Hobart, Baron Hobart and Governor of Madras 1794–8. It is inscribed on the back, 'Drawn from recollection at Madras 1793', and shows Smart's ability to memorize a likeness.

In 1796 he drew what is, in my opinion, one of his finest and most exquisite portraits of children, that of his grandchild, Robert Woolf, then a boy of 10, dressed in a pale-blue tunic with his fair hair falling over a white collar. With his usual thoroughness Smart wrote on the back instructions as to how it should be hung in the room in order that the drawing might be appreciated to the full.

Smart painted a particularly charming portrait of Anne, Marchioness Townsend, signed and dated 1775.[1] This portrait is perfectly placed within its frame; the dark, almost drab background, simple dress and high coiffeur illustrates to perfection the painter's ability to portray a likeness, to model the features and to produce an outstanding portrait without recourse to extraneous and unnecessary detail.

Smart seldom painted miniatures of women with their hats on, two exceptions being those of Mrs Lewin, painted in 1784, and Mrs (later Lady) Oakeley, painted in India in 1786, which are both attractive and graceful. Miniatures of Indian women painted by Smart are rarely seen and no sketches depicting any have so far come to light. Two miniatures exist, one of a beautiful Indian girl, possibly one of the Nawab of Arcot's household, signed and dated 1790, and now in Lord Wharton's collection; the other, also of a young woman, was contained in the lid of an ivory snuff box. This had a secret spring, which, when pressed, opened the lid and revealed the portrait, and it may well have been associated with some hidden romance.

An interesting collection of drawings of the Wigram family by Smart was sold by a descendant, the Rev. Sir Clifford Wigram, in June 1959. The portrait of Sir Robert Wigram, 1st Baronet of Wexford, and that of his son, Robert Fitzwigram, 2nd Baronet, were both signed and dated 1805. Some of the drawings were heightened with colour and were from 4½ in. to 8½ in. in size. Of the twelve drawings sold, five of them were groups, portraying nineteen of Sir Robert Wigram's twenty-three children and

[1] 2nd wife of 4th Viscount m. on 19 May 1773. Created Marquess 31 October 1787.

the second Lady Wigram.[1] Sir Robert was a merchant and was created a baronet in 1805; his first wife was Catherine Brodhurst, who died in 1786, and his second wife, whom he married in 1787, died in 1841, having survived him by eleven years. All the drawings were superb and, as far as is known, this was the only collection depicting almost an entire family.

Smart is reputed to have become friendly with the son of a London jeweller, Augustus Toussaint, who had been apprenticed to James Nixon, A.R.A., the miniaturist. Toussaint was himself both a miniaturist and jeweller, who devoted much of his time to designing elaborate miniature frames. Dr Williamson refers to Smart having employed him to make several special frames, including the one which contained the portrait of his son, John, who had died in infancy.

There were two artists, apart from Smart's son, who imitated his style very closely. Samuel Andrews, who also worked in India, was certainly one of his followers. He arrived in Madras in 1791 and, after Smart's departure for England, announced that 'he had taken a house in North Street, Madras, lately occupied by Mr Smart, and would attend to all orders for miniatures'.[2] For many years portraits signed 'S.A.' have been attributed to Sarah Addington, but recently several signed works by Samuel Andrews have come to light and it is now thought that those formerly attributed to Miss Addington were, in all probability, the work of Andrews. Another artist whose work is occasionally confused with that of Smart is James Scouler, who shared a similar signature and at the outset copied Smart's style. The majority of his miniatures are much weaker, in both draughtsmanship and colouring, but early works by this artist have not infrequently been attributed to Smart.

Notwithstanding the excellence of all Smart's miniatures, his finest period was certainly that between 1775 and 1800, when he was at the height of his powers and produced portraits which were among the finest ever executed by any artist of the eighteenth century.

[1] A family group comprising Sir R. Wigram and his 2nd wife Eleanor, 14 sons, 5 daughters, and 2 brothers was engraved by C. TURNER, 1826.
[2] *Walpole Society*, Vol. XIX, p. 8.

CHAPTER FIVE

The Smart Family

AFTER MANY years' research on the part of a number of people, it is now possible to place on record a considerable amount of information about Smart's family—information which in many cases alters completely much of what has been previously written.

The almost total absence of any records has made the task of piecing together all the various threads of evidence very difficult. Indeed, even now many of the vital links are still elusive. Nevertheless the details that have emerged make it clear that Smart and his family kept in close contact with each other during his lifetime, and one can only regret that no diary or letters have so far come to light to clear up the mystery of his birth and parentage. In order to clarify the family history it is necessary to repeat here some details already referred to.

Smart made three marriages, the first to a lady whose name is so far unknown, but who later deserted him for William Pars. By this marriage he had a son John and two daughters, Anna Maria and Sophia. His second marriage was to Edith (Vere?), by whom as far as is known he had no issue.[1] Smart finally married Mary Morton, by whom he had a son, John James. In addition he had issue out of wedlock by Sarah Midgeley: namely a daughter Sarah, and a son John, who, as has already been stated, was the one who followed his father's profession.[2]

John, the son of Smart's first marriage, was probably born about 1762, judging by a miniature painted by his father in 1765, when the boy appears to be about 3 years of age. This portrait was illustrated by Dr G. C. Williamson and was formerly in the collection of Mr E. M. Hodgkinson.[3] As there is no record of his existence later, and as the son born out of

[1] Williamson, *Portrait Miniatures*, London, 1897, p. 49.
[2] Chancery Court Proceedings, 1790.
[3] Now in the National Museum, Stockholm.

wedlock was named John and took his father's name, one can only con-
clude that the boy died young. He could not have been the John Smart,
Junior, who followed his father's profession as a miniaturist, and the
portrait referred to above is the only known reference to his existence.

Anna Maria (1766–1813), who accompanied her father to India in
1785, married, on 11 July 1786, Robert, son of David Woolf, a merchant
of London. Anna died on 17 November 1813, and her husband on
1 January 1836, having married as his second wife Hester Shaw, who
survived him and by whom he had six children, Harri, Charles, Frederick,
Alfred and Hester (twins) and Edward.[1]

By his first wife Anna Maria, Robert Woolf had nine children, Robert
(1786?–1825), Anna Sophia (1789–1840), Elizabeth Anne (b. 1790),
Anna Carolina (b. 1792), Maria (b. 1793), John William (b. Jan./Feb.
1795–1869), William Henry (b. 1800), George Balfour (b. 1801) and
Charlotte Emma (1803–1865).

According to an old diary kept by Robert Woolf, and at one time in
the possession of one of his descendants, the Woolf family were left in
straitened circumstances when his father died, due to Mrs Woolf being
defrauded by her late husband's partner. Robert was placed in a merchant's counting-house with Sir G. Wombell, where he worked until
1775, when as a boy of only 19 he was sent to Boston with £4,000 or
£5,000 in dollars to pay some of the King's Troop stationed there,
arriving just before the Battle of Bunker Hill. Two years later Woolf
returned to England, and in 1779 he entered the Madras Civil Service,
becoming successively Auditor of Civil Accounts and Deputy Auditor
in 1791, and Accountant-General in 1795.

Mrs Woolf and four of her children left Madras in October 1794, but
remained at St Helena for some months owing to the birth of her sixth
child, John William. The family re-embarked on the *Melville Castle* on
5 September 1795, reaching England in November. It is not known
where the Woolf family lived when they arrived in London, but they
may well have gone to Smart's house in Grafton Street, for which he had
been paying rent since 1790.

Also in his diary, Robert Woolf refers to his wife's return to Madras
in 1798.[2] A seventh child, William Henry, was born to them in 1800
and baptized on 14 February of that year, and another son, George
Balfour, was born in Madras and baptized on 16 May 1801. On 29
December 1865, at Bromley, Kent, the death occurred of Charlotte

[1] *Jaffé Papers.*
[2] *Grindon Papers.*

Emma, aged 62, daughter of Robert and Anna Woolf. No details of her birth have been found, but it must have been in 1803, after the family had returned from India, and she could have been only about 10 years old when her mother died. Anna Maria Woolf was buried on 17 November 1813, in the Clifton Churchyard, Bristol, being then 47 years of age.

On 9 December 1799, Robert Woolf opened an account at Coutts Bank in London into which he paid £1,598. 8s. and soon afterwards bought stock to the value of £1,584. 10s. 6d. He paid in considerable sums of money, from time to time, and bought large amounts of stock. Between April 1801 and June 1802 sums amounting to £1,120 were paid to Elizabeth Woolf (1748–1828), who may well have been responsible for looking after the Woolf children during the absence of their parents.[1] She was their aunt, and in one place is referred to as Mrs Woolf, whilst one of the family records show her as Robert's sister.

In 1802, Woolf paid £150 to John Smart on 10 February, and on 26 April a further £200, the day on which Smart himself opened an account at Coutts with £150. By July 1802, Robert Woolf and his wife were back in England, for he withdrew £100 from Coutts on 17 July and a further £100 on 31 July, and from then onwards was withdrawing money regularly. A further £300 was paid to Smart on 19 August 1802 and on 29 September £80.[2]

From entries in Woolf's diary for 1802 it would appear that, on reaching England, he went to live at Hampstead, but after February 1804 money was frequently sent him by post to Leigh House, near Bradford-on-Avon. On 21 June 1808 he mortgaged this estate to John Smart for £600 with his brother William and Robert Bowyer acting as trustees. The interest on the £600 was to be paid to Sarah Smart, together with the interest on a substantial sum in bank annuities which Smart also placed in trust for Sarah's benefit.[3] Robert Woolf had retired from the Madras Civil Service on a pension in 1802 or 1803, but from 16th February 1832 until 1 January 1836, the year of his death, he was in receipt of a compassionate allowance of £2. 2s. per week from the Madras Civil Fund.

Robert, the eldest son, seems to have been a considerable favourite with his family, as is evidenced by an inscription on the back of a portrait of him, painted by his grandfather. The date of his birth is uncertain, but details written on the reverse of a miniature owned by a descendant of

---

[1] Messrs Coutts & Co.
[2] Messrs Coutts & Co.
[3] *Busteed Papers.* (See Chapter V, re Sarah Smart.)

the family, Mrs Mabel Hughes, give the date as February 1786, and state that he was baptized at St Mary's Church, Madras, 10 March, 1786.[1] However, his application for a cadetship, preserved at the India Office, records his baptism as 16 June 1787.[2] The superb miniature of him by Smart, already referred to, was sold at Sotheby's on 11 July 1960. On the back of this portrait a lengthy inscription supports the date of 1786 as his natal year and states that he was educated in London. The description of the miniature of Master Robert Woolf given in Sotheby's Catalogue is as follows:

A FINE AND ATTRACTIVE MINIATURE OF MASTER ROBERT WOOLF, *by John Smart, signed and dated July 16th, 1796, nearly half-length, head and shoulders three-quarters dexter, gaze directed at spectator, his fair hair falling to a white collar over his pale blue tunic, painted on paper within a feigned circle and signed in full at the base, the back also with a long and detailed inscription, now somewhat worn but transcribed below, rectangular, 6¾ in., in gilt-wood frame, 9¼ in.*

'*Beware of what the world calls happiness—all this died with thee dear Robert.*'

Portrait of } *Jonny*
Master Robert Woolf } *a lovely boy*
  an affectionate brother
  and a dutiful child
age ten years the 16th April 1796
born at Madras April 1786
died at Jalnah September 1825
educated in London
the most beloved and } *Captn of Cavalry eldest son of*
most affectionate brother } *Robt Woolf Esq. of Madras*
of Mrs J. B. Grindon }
To be hung on that side of the room as you stand with your left arm towards the window, otherwise it will appear rougher from the unevenness of the paper it is painted on and always to be viewed in the same manner.
  painted by his grandfather
  J. Smart[3]
London, July 16th, 1796.

As the portrait was executed by Smart in England, on 16 April 1796, when Woolf was 10 years of age, it is evident that the boy was sent to England before his mother returned from India, for his name is not recorded as accompanying her on the voyage home.

Robert Woolf became a cadet in 1803 and was later advanced to

[1] *Grindon Papers.*
[2] India Office, Cadet Papers, 281, 1804, Commonwealth Relations Office.
[3] Sotheby's Catalogue of 11 July 1960.

Captain in the 6th Madras Light Cavalry, and died at Jalnah on 29 September 1825. He is known to have married Augusta Ann Green, who, as a widow, was admitted a pensioner of Lord Clive's Fund, 4 April 1827, but was struck out of the lists on her second marriage, 5 October 1827. Robert Woolf and Augusta had no children.

Anna Sophia was the eldest daughter of Robert and Anna Maria and married Joseph Baker Grindon (1790–1870) on 28 September 1815 at St Nicholas Church, Uphill, Somerset. They had eight children, Julia Bailward, Leopold Hartley, Cornelia, Sophia, Hamilton Edmund, Arthur St Ledger, Joseph Russell, and Octavius Maunsell. Anna Sophia is said to have ridden to church on her wedding day dressed in a green riding habit. The couple later went to stay at Uphill Castle.

The Grindon family came from Bristol, where Joseph was Coroner and a much-respected citizen of that city. One of their sons, Leo Grindon, became a well-known author and lecturer in Manchester.

In a letter written to Hamilton Edmund Grindon, one of her eight children, Anna Sophia, mentions that Robert Woolf had lent £90,000 to the Rajah of Mysore, who after a period of three years ceased to pay the interest. The letter goes on to say that on his return from India, Woolf had bought Uphill Castle, 'near Weston Super Mare, twenty miles from Bristol'.[1] Arthur de Grindon, another descendant, writing to Mr Jaffé in 1946, says: 'It is not a Castle, but a great rambling castle-like Victorian Mansion.'[2] There is no conclusive evidence of Woolf's purchase, but a later owner found in one of the cellars a small pot with the name 'Woolf' upon it. A daughter, Cornelia, who married Henry William Tippett in a letter to her brother, Arthur St Ledger Grindon, in 1886, describes the house at Bradford where the grandparents lived.

Apparently another daughter, Sophia Grindon, had visited the old family home and gone to see their brother Octavius, who was by this time the Rector of South Wraxall, a village only three miles from Bradford-on-Avon. Sophia explains that as there was only a dog cart at South Wraxall they were obliged to hire a coach from Bradford to take them to the Rectory. 'Bradford,' she says, 'is a nice clean, quiet, old-fashioned town, hilly, with narrow winding streets, and a few shops with necessities; they go to Bath for their chief commodities.'

The old house had been renamed 'Fairfield', and the grounds considerably altered, although the house remained unchanged, but in the village, the broad open downs of which their mother had often spoken

[1] *Grindon Papers.*
[2] *Jaffé Papers.*

had been cut up with roads and fences. Sophia remarked on the Agapanthus blooming on either side of the Rectory door; the root she says had been brought from the Cape by Robert Woolf, on his voyage home in 1802.[1]

Maria, fourth daughter of Robert and Anna, died in Ohio, U.S.A. She married a James Holbrook, by whom she had three children, Charles, James, and Aquilla.

John William, the second son, married Mary Ann Carpenter, by whom he had the following children—Marianne Caroline, John, Hamilton Edmund, and Susan Augusta, who died in 1867. Of the other children of Robert Woolf and Anna Maria Smart, nothing is known.

Woolf did not remain at Leigh House after his first wife's death, although he evidently remained in the area, as his daughter, Sophia, was married from Uphill, in 1815; while Cowslip Lodge, Batcombe Court, Somerset, and Highbridge House, Dundry, near Bristol, are all mentioned in his diary as places where he resided.[2]

Evidence that Robert Woolf married a second time is to be found in an obituary notice published in *The Times* on 25 July 1864: 'At Upper Norwood, aged 36, Esther, youngest daughter of the late Robert Woolf, Esq: Accountant General at Madras.' This fact is confirmed by an entry in his diary for 1816, and the Grindon family tree supplies the name of Hester Shaw as his second wife, by whom he had six children, and Hester, not Esther, as the name of the daughter who is undoubtedly the one referred to in the obituary notice. Robert died at Turnham Green on 2 or 11 March 1836, and was buried at Chiswick aged 81.

Sophia, younger daughter of John Smart by his first wife, was born in 1770 and died in 1793. After her sister, Anna Maria's, marriage, Sophia joined her father in India and married, on 8 February 1790, John, a posthumous child of John Dighton of Clifford Chambers, Gloucestershire, by Elizabeth, daughter of John Hunter. He was the tenth child of the marriage and was born in 1761. He became a lieutenant in the Army in 1784, attaining the rank of lieutenant-general in 1837. Sophia Dighton died in 1793, apparently in childbed, having given birth to a son John. Lieutenant Dighton married secondly, on 22 October 1795 at Masulipatam, Miss Boyd, about whom nothing is known. Evidence of this marriage is to be found in the *Madras Courier*, Vol. XI, Wednesday, 9 December 1795: 'At Masulipatam on 22nd October Lieutenant John Dighton to Miss Boyd.' Dighton married thirdly, Arabella Veronica

[1] *Grindon Papers.*
[2] *Grindon Papers.*

Mein, daughter of Surgeon Mein, by whom he had further issue—Charles Mein (1797-1826), David Boyd (1798-1824), Richard Henry (1799-1854), James Anderson (? died young), Robert (1804-1826), and John (d. 1811, aged 14 days).

Charles entered the Army, but later took Holy Orders. He married Maria Probyn, daughter of the Rev. John Probyn, and had three children —John Henry, Charles Edward, and Veronica Arabella. David Boyd became lieutenant in Madras Artillery, and was killed in action at the Siege of Kittore, on 22 October 1824. Richard Henry went to India, where he remained for some years; he never married and died at Newland, Gloucestershire, on 2 December 1854. According to the family history, both James and Robert died young, but this must be an error, for Robert's death is recorded in the *Gentleman's Magazine* as taking place in London on 29 January 1826. John died fourteen days after his birth and was buried on 19 October 1811 in the grave of his grandfather, Nichol Mein, at Madras.

Miniatures of the three elder sons are illustrated in *The Dightons of Clifford Chambers*[1] written by one of their descendants, and the baptism of these three is recorded as taking place at St Mary's Church, Madras, on 3 August 1801.

John Dighton (then Major-General) married fourthly, in January 1821, Susan Probyn, the third daughter of Edmund Probyn of Newland, Gloucestershire. She died on 20 May 1862, aged 93, and he, at Gloucester, on 13 June 1840. A mural tablet commemorating him and his fourth wife is in the King Edward's Chantry of Newland Parish Church.

Sacred to the Memory of
Lieut. General John Dighton
of the Hon. East India Comp's Service
Madras Establishment
who departed this life June 13th, 1840
(aged 79 years)
also
Susan, relict of the above
Lieut. Gen. John Dighton
and third daughter of Edmund Probyn Esq.
of Newland
who departed this life May 20th, 1862
aged 93 years.
'*I will ransome them from the power of the grave*
I will redeem them from death'

Hosea XIII 14.

[1] Dighton, Conway, *The Dightons of Clifford Chambers*, London, 1902.

Sophia, John Dighton's first wife, died and was buried at Muticore, west of Kistnapatam, the following inscription being placed upon her tomb—

> *Sacred*
> *To the memory of*
> *Mrs Sophia Dighton who departed*
> *This life on the 2nd of June 1793*
> *Aged 23 years*
> *Wife to Lieut. John Dighton*
> *The Hon'ble Company's Service.*
> *Her virtues*
> *Were eminently conspicuous*
> *discreet*
> *in all her actions, amiable*
> *and affectionate*
> *Wife.*

The tomb is mentioned in the list of European Tombs in the Nellore District, to the south of Kistnapatam, which is on the banks of the Buckingham Canal in the Nellore District.[1]

John Dighton, only son of Lieutenant John Dighton by his wife, Sophia Smart, was baptized on 20 May 1794 at St Mary's Church, Fort St George, and after his mother's death was brought to England under the care of his aunt, Mrs Robert Woolf, and must have grown up with her children. His grandfather made a sketch of him on paper, on the back of which is written: 'John Dighton aged eleven years, born at Multicore (100 miles North of Madras) June 4th 1793, and my grandson and painted by me, John Smart.' The boy died at sea when he was only 17 years of age whilst on his way out to India as a cadet for the Madras Army.

By his association with Sarah Midgeley, John Smart, who had been deserted by his first wife and left with his two small daughters, Anna Maria and Sophia, aged about 9 and 5 years respectively had a daughter, Sarah, and a son, John,[2] as has been already mentioned.

John was born in 1776 and was the only child to follow his father's profession; details of his life are given in a separate chapter. He died in 1809 at Madras.

Sarah, his sister, was born in 1781 and died on 2 February 1853. Little is known about her except that she was living in her father's house before his last marriage and continued to do so for several years. Smart then made provision for Sarah to find other accommodation. Evidence for this provision has come to my notice among some family papers owned

[1] *Jaffé Papers.*
[2] Chancery Court Proceedings, 1790.

by Mr J. W. Busteed, great-great-grandson of the artist. It is contained in an indenture, made on 27 May 1808 and signed on 21 June 1808, between John Smart, William Woolf of the Middle Temple (Robert's brother), Robert Bowyer of Pall Mall,[1] and Sarah Smart, whose address was then given as 2 Russell Place, and she was stated to be 'residing with, and the daughter of said John Smart'. Farington in his *Diary* of 1810 mentions that Nollekens said: Smart has settled £100 a year upon His daughter who has retired from His House, & left Him to live with His young wife.'[2]

As has already been mentioned, Robert Woolf had mortgaged his estate at Bradford Leigh to William Woolf and Robert Bowyer for the sum of £600, which was paid by John Smart, who also placed £1,750 in 4 per cent Consolidated Bank Annuities in trust for Sarah. William Woolf and Robert Bowyer were appointed trustees to pay any interest and dividends to Sarah or anyone whom she appointed on condition that it was neither sold nor mortgaged. In the case of her marrying it was to be paid for her separate use, and on her separate receipt.

Upon Sarah's death the £600 principal money and the £1,750 4 per cent Annuities, together with the future interest and dividends, were to be left in trust for all, or any one or more of her children, in such proportions as she should think fit, and by any deed or by her will direct. In case she should leave no direction, then it would be left in trust for all her children equally.

In the event of Sarah marrying and having no children, half the trust fund was to be paid to her executors or administrators, and the other half to return to John Smart's estate. Should it be necessary a sum of up to £500 could be advanced to Sarah at any time and her half of the trust fund reduced proportionately. Should she die unmarried, then the trust was to pay her executors £500 and the residue of the trust fund was to return to John Smart's estate. A covenant was also made by John Smart to pay the property and income tax during Sarah's lifetime.

Nothing more is known about Sarah Midgeley, the mother of John and Sarah, beyond the fact that Smart, during his absence in India, made ample provision for her and the children, and as no mention is made of her later the presumption is that she died before his return to England.

It was in about 1799 that Smart married Edith (Vere?), by whom, as far as is known, he had no issue, and about whom nothing is known. His

---

[1] Robert Bowyer (1758?–1834) had been guardian to Sarah and John, Junior, when Smart was in India.
[2] *Farington Diary*, Greig Edit., Vol. VI, p. 10.

13   14
15   16

PLATE FOUR

third and last marriage was to Mary Morton (1783–1851) and took place on 14 February 1805, when she was 22 years of age. They continued to live at 2 Russell Place, where their son, John James (1805–70), was born on 7 October 1805. He married Elizabeth Bailey and had one child, a daughter, Mary Ann (1856–1934). A miniature of John, painted by his father in 1807, was sold from the Dyer Collection; it was set in an oval pearl frame and shows him to have been a fine-looking child, with features very like those of his mother.[1] John Smart made ample provision for this son under his will. He received £1,000 on attaining the age of 21 and inherited his father's estate on the death of his mother, on 24 September 1851, and a further legacy of £1,839. 2s. 4d. on the death of his half-sister, Sarah, who died a spinster on 2 February 1853. A receipt for the legacy from his father, signed by John James, is as follows:

Received this 24th day of April, 1828, the Sum of Thirteen Hundred and Twenty Pounds Stock 3½ Per Cent Consolidated Bank Annuities (the same having been transferred into my name in the Books of the Bank of England) in full discharge of the Legacy of One Thousand Pounds payable to me under the Will of my late Father John Smart, and all claims and demands whatsoever in respect thereof.

J. J. SMART.

When John James and his wife were first married they lived in a house called the Poplars, at Brook Street, a small village near Brentwood, now on the main Romford-Brentwood road. From there they moved to a house they named Balgores, situated at Hare Street, near Romford, now called Gidea Park. There was a smaller house in existence, some 65 acres in all, including gardens, fields, a coachman's cottage and land which went as far as the railway line.

As a result of an appeal for information about John Smart, Mr Jaffé received a letter written by a lady who came from Worthing, and who had in her possession several interesting relics of the artist which included the following articles:

A sketch for a miniature with the name 'Sharnacks' written underneath in pencil, another of a baby, a signed sketch of the Common, Tunbridge Wells by Mrs Smart, and an old engraving on India paper, commemorating the Jubilee of George III in 1810, on which is written in ink in Smart's handwriting, 'John James Smart was breeched Thursday'. The lady also had some old oval cards which he used for sketches, an engraving of one of his portraits of a boy, and an old plan of the house that John James had altered at Romford, showing ponds, brewery, stables, lake,

---

[1] This miniature is now in the collection of Mrs E. Holzscheiter of Zurich.

etc. The letter had been written to a lady whose name was not given, and the author of the letter could not be traced when Mr Jaffé made inquiries in 1941. When the Smarts took the property they enlarged the house on either side, no doubt according to the plans referred to, and it was added to again when his daughter went to live there after her father's death.

A diary of the year 1867 written by John James has been preserved and from it we learn that he and his family were devout church people, who worshipped regularly at Romford Church and had family prayers.

Their only child, Mary Ann, who was at this time 11 years old and to whom John James was obviously devoted, was attending a boarding school at Brentwood, run by a Miss Jackson. Mary was usually rather homesick and returned to school with reluctance!

After the death of his mother, Mary Caley, his stepfather continued to live with them. He was in poor health and advancing years, which necessitated the attendance of a nurse, who looked after him with the help of the family. He was in receipt of a War Office Superannuation which his stepson fetched from London on his frequent visits. On 14 November 1867 John James mentions friends coming to wish his stepfather a 'Happy Birthday' and says '89th year'. The old man died in 1868, only two years before John James himself, who had also been unwell on and off for some time, and had been under a Dr Grimwood of London, a family friend.

John James Smart died on 26 September 1870, and it is therefore impossible for him to have been the person referred to by Redgrave and Basil Long as committing suicide in 1856. He and his wife, as well as his mother and stepfather, Mr Caley, were all buried at South Weald, a village near Brentwood and a short distance from Brook Street. The following inscriptions, which are now indecipherable owing to the weathering of the stone, were on the tombstones:

1.
Sacred to the memory of
Mary, the beloved wife of
Mr John Sidey Caley, of this parish
Who departed this life
September 24th 1851
aged 68 years
Requiescat in pace

Also of the above

Mr John Sidey Caley
Who departed this life
Oct 12th 1868
Aged 90 years.

2.
> *In affectionate remembrance*
> *of John James Smart of*
> *Hare St Romford,*
> *Late of Brook St in this parish,*
> *Who departed this life*
> *September 26th 1870*
> *In the 65th year of his life.*

Also of

> *Elizabeth, wife of the above who*
> *departed this life,*
> *November 27th 1893*
> *In the 83rd year of her age.*

The parish records show that Mary Caley, who died intestate, was buried on 2 October 1851 and her husband on 17 October 1868, and give his age as 89. According to the parish register, John James was buried on 4 October 1870.[1]

The following letter relates to his parents' deaths:

Dear Sir,

In reply to your request I beg to inform you that my dear mother departed this life, September 24th 1851 and my father May 1st 1811.

> *I am,*
> *Dear Sir*
> *Yours truly,*
> J. J. SMART

Brook St
Brentwood
Essex.
April 26th 1853.   Mr B. Engleheart, Esq.[2]

Among the papers retained by the Busteed family is some correspondence between Edward Smirke, afterwards Sir Edward Smirke (1795–1875) and John James Smart.

Sarah Smart was a friend of Mary Smirke (d. 1853), Sir Edward's sister, to whom she had evidently given a portrait of her father, some pictures and a book containing a number of miniatures. After Miss Smirke's death her brother offered to return the portrait to the family, as is seen by the following letters, which also refer to some stock which had belonged to Sarah Smart and was transferred by Edward Smirke to John James.

[1] Parish Records and Tombs seen 1961.
[2] *Busteed Papers.*

3 King's Bench Walks,
Temple.
28 Oct.

Sir,

On looking over the effects of my late sister, I find a few articles formerly belonging to her friend Miss Smart—among them is a remarkably good picture, containing a portrait (as I am informed) of Mr Smart, your father.

As it is a remarkably good painting and a very pleasing picture, I have put it aside in case you should wish to possess it.

If it should only be a duplicate of one in your possession, it will of course have little value, but I shall at all events be glad to hand it to you or to any other member of the family, if desired, and will send it to any person in town whom you may name.

I think there are two other small pictures, which she gave to my sister, but I do not think they are worth mentioning to you, or that you would care to possess them.

I am Sir,
faithfully yrs.,
E. SMIRKE

Fri. This morning I attended to transfer the settled stock, late of Miss Smart's, into your name and to hand over the two last dividends to your agent, Mr Fuller.

J. Smart, Esq.

Sir,

I feel greatly obliged for your kind remembrance of me, in preserving and offering the Portrait of my Father, the property of the late Miss Smart and shall have great pleasure in accepting it.

Will cheerfully accept your offer to forward it to Messrs Fuller's and Saltwell's offices, Carlton Chambers, at your convenience.

The first time when in town, will accept the Stock, late Miss Smart's, which you inform me, you have transferred into my name, and for which I beg to tender my best thanks.

I am Sir,
faithfully yours,
J. J. SMART

E. Smirke, Esq.

Dear Sir,

Calling yesterday upon Mr Fuller, he kindly presented your most valuable and spontaneous gift, a portrait of my late dear Father, to me of intrinsic worth, not having a similar one in my possession, and decidedly a very correct and pleasing representation.

I trust to be permitted to express my sincere thanks for all favors bestowed and to heartily wish a continuation of health and happiness for many years.

> *Believe me,*
> *My dear Sir,*
> *Yours faithfully,*
> J. J. SMART

Brook Street
Dec. 13th 1853
E. Smirke, Esq.

The portrait referred to was an oil painting of John Smart, originally attributed to Sir Joshua Reynolds, but when it was sold at Sotheby's in 1934 it was re-attributed to Gilbert Stuart and is now in the Joslyn Art Museum, Omaha.

In the *Gentleman's Magazine* for 1853 is recorded the death on 14 September of Miss Smirke of Grove Road, Slough. On Mary's death the book containing the miniatures went to another of Mary's brothers, Sidney Smirke, R.A. (1798–1878), who left them divided between two of his daughters, Mrs Mary O. Jemmett, wife of the Rev. J. F. Jemmett, and Mrs Lange. These miniatures were exhibited at the Royal Amateur Art Society Exhibition of 1904. In a letter dated 1928, Mrs Jemmett said her collection was sold at Christie's on 29 February of that year, but there is reason for thinking that part of it may have been sold earlier. After Mrs Lange's death, her brother Edward sold her collection at Christie's on 10 December 1928.

Mary Ann Smart, the only child of John James and his wife Elizabeth, was born at Brook Street on 9 June 1856. She married William Bose, by whom she had four children—William, Lilian, Mabel, and Winnie. Mary Ann died at Worthing in April 1934 and William Bose in 1929. When the family were living at Brook Street her father commenced the alterations of the house, and a foundation stone was laid by her on 15 May 1865, which is inscribed as follows:

> *This*
> *Foundation Stone was laid*
> *By Miss Mary Ann Smart*
> *on May 15th 1865*
> *in the presence of her parents*
> J. J. & E. SMART
>
> *Also*
> MR THORNE
> MR COOPER
> MR BROWN
> MISS L. WADSWORTH

J. S. CALEY, ESQ.
R. HUNT, LIEUT. COL.
W. COOPER, ESQ.
S. BROWN, ESQ.

MR F. THORNE   J. S. HAMMOND
Architect   *Builder*
London.   *Romford.*

This stone may still be seen in the basement of the house, which is now called 'Gidea Park College', but owing to the crumbling of the surface the inscription is now almost indistinguishable.[1]

The premises are now used as a mixed school for about 200 children, aged between 5 and 11. The house seems to have remained unchanged, and although much of the land has been disposed of, it stands in spacious grounds in which the stables and coach-house are still to be seen. A splendid cedar tree stands near the house on the south side, from which a lawn spreads out for some distance beyond.

The rooms are lofty and mostly square in shape, many of them having the original fireplaces which are placed under the window, a device seldom seen nowadays. The upstairs rooms are placed in suites with two or three leading off each other, and the house, in spite of its size, gives the impression of being homely and welcoming.

In a letter to Mr Arthur Jaffé in 1941, the Rev. G. Montagu Benton, Hon. Sec. and Editor of the Essex Archaeological Society, describes how his wife, whose home was near that of the Smart family at Balgores, often played with the Bose children, 'Lilian, Mabel, Winnie and a boy (named after his father William)'; and remembers Mrs Smart, a dear old lady who made her home with Mrs Bose and her family after her husband's death.[2] In the Smarts' lifetime the village was called Hare Street and next to their house was a delightful old cottage, called Repton, so named after its owner, Humphrey Repton, the famous eighteenth-century landscape gardener. Mr and Mrs Bose continued to live at Balgores until about 1910, when finding the neighbourhood was becoming suburban, they sold the property to the Gidea Park Estate, who in turn sold it to its present owners, Gidea Park College. The Bose's spent the rest of their lives in hotels.

Among the Smart relics owned by Mrs Bose was a cornelian seal that had belonged to John Smart, the engraving on it being the same as that on the medals made by Kirk.

---

[1] Seen in 1961.
[2] *Jaffé Papers.*

After the death of Mrs Bose a number of her possessions were sold at Worthing on 17 and 18 July 1934. These included thirty-five miniatures by John Smart, two bronze medals of Smart, and seventeen Hornchurch $\frac{1}{2}$ tokens of the late eighteenth century. Also included in the sale was a beautiful travelling sundial $4\frac{1}{4}$ in. by $4\frac{1}{2}$ in., by John Gilbert of Tower Hill, London, and once the property of John Smart. It was made about 1775 and had a fine brass dial with a revolving centrepiece and a compass with a silver dial. It was in perfect condition, and was contained in the original shagreen case with Gilbert's trade label still on it. The sundial and compass, together with a set of drawing instruments, only fetched thirty shillings.

It is through the families of John James Smart that many of the sketches and miniatures executed by John Smart have descended. Mary Ann, who had married William Bose, left her possessions divided between her family, William H. Bose, Lilian, wife of Mr Dyer, Mabel, wife of Dr J. H. Busteed, and Blanche Winifred, wife of Percy Shepheard. This last daugher did not inherit any sketches or miniatures from her parents, but had her share of the estate in money.

Many of the sketches sold by the family had details of sitters and other information written on them by Smart, and it was unfortunate that they were dispersed before any of these facts could be recorded.

The Bose collection was sold at Christie's on 15 February 1937, the Dyer collection on 17 December 1936, and the Busteed collection on 26 November 1937. Mrs Dyer, who for some years lived at Bexhill, named her house 'Balgores' after the family home.[1] Several hundred sketches were disposed of in these sales and some of them reappear in the sale-rooms from time to time and are very desirable. Unfortunately, much of the information connected with them has now been lost, and they are now so widely scattered that it would be impossible to obtain it again.

From the facts that have come to light during the course of my research on the large and scattered family stemming from the great miniaturist, it is quite clear that, in spite of the numerous marriages within the family, Smart was loved and respected by them all, and the various branches were in close contact with each other during his lifetime. Although Smart was a much-married man, and one who was attracted to women, he was devoted to his children and grandchildren; and notwithstanding the one-sided assessment of his character given in Thomas Jones's *Diary*, one is disposed to agree with the late Mr Arthur Jaffé when he said that he was a 'good husband, father and grandfather'.

[1] Present descendants of the family still reside at Bexhill.

CHAPTER SIX

John Smart, Junior (1776–1809)

JOHN SMART, Junior, was not, as has always been stated, the offspring of his father's first marriage, the child of that marriage—also named John—having died in infancy, but was a natural son of John Smart and Sarah Midgeley.

Of the mother's life, history and background nothing is known, nor what became of her after Smart went to India. Evidence of her connexion with him is to be found in the Proceedings of the Chancery Court for 13 February 1790, already referred to in Chapter One.

It will be remembered that before leaving England, Smart had placed his family in the guardianship of Thomas Parkinson and Philip Paumier, and in an indenture dated 26 March 1785 he assigned property in Water Lane, Fleet Street, London, on trust for the use of Sarah Midgeley and the two children, and further arranged for some portion of the rents and profits of the estate to be used for the children's education and maintenance. Smart must have kept in close touch with the family, and from what news he had of their progress became dissatisfied with the way in which his trust was being administered. He did not approve of the school to which Sarah had been sent and took steps to see that the situation did not continue. No mention is made of the boy's schooling, but on 14 October 1788, Smart executed a Deed-Poll at Fort St George, appointing Robert Bowyer and Edmund Monk as joint attorneys to manage his estate and superintend the children's education; they were also empowered to settle his account with Thomas Parkinson and Philip Paumier, the two previous guardians. He desired his attorneys to place the children in 'such schools or Academies' as they should think fit and to take care of them. The matter came before the Chancery Court on 5 March 1790, when letters by John Smart, which have not been preserved, were produced, and the Master, Edward Montague, agreed to the change of guardianship.

During his time in India, in addition to the arrangements for the maintenance and guardianship of the children, Smart appears to have provided also for their accommodation, at all events he paid the rates for No. 20 Grafton Street from 1790 onwards, and it is probable that this house was the family home before the move to Russell Place. The boy would have been 8 years old and his sister about 4 years old when their father left for India in 1785.

While it is possible that the younger Smart studied under Daniel Dodd, he could not have been the Master Smart who exhibited as his pupil at the Free Society of Artists in 1770, nor the one who entered portraits at the Society of Artists in 1775 and 1776. This artist was in all probability the John Smart who was working in Ipswich 1786–7, but about whom practically nothing is known. Smart did, however, exhibit at the Royal Academy from 1800 until his death. There is no indication at present as to where John was educated, but evidence that he was taught miniature painting by his father is contained in a letter written by John Smart to the Honourable Court of Directors of the East India Company on 28 May 1808, as follows:

May 28th 1808
Russell Place
Fitzroy Square

Honorable Sirs,
Having been pleased formerly to allow me to go to India to follow my profession of a miniature painter. I respectfully solicit the same indulgence for my son John Smart who has been taught by me and has obtained a proficiency in the same line that will do honour to me and credit to himself under the circumstances. I humbly beg leave to express my hope that your honorable Court will condescend to grant permission to my Son to follow the same profession of a Miniature painter only which can be inserted in the body of the Covenant and that he may proceed to India by the earliest opportunity.

I have the honour to be
with the highest respect
Honorable Sirs
Your greatly obliged
and very humble Servant
JOHN SMART

The Honorable the
 Court of Directors of
  the East India Company.

Dr G. C. Williamson has said that in the course of his research at the Convent at Lodi into the life of Richard Cosway, he found evidence that John Smart, Senior, was for a time a pupil of Cosway's and that he referred to him as 'Honest John' and 'Good Little John'.[1] It is now generally accepted that the author must have been mistaken or have drawn an erroneous conclusion from the material before him. It is possible that John Smart, Junior, in his father's absence, was taught by Cosway, but so far there is no evidence for this. There were several artists bearing the same name and in almost every case their history is obscure.

The young Smart was evidently still living with his father at 2 Russell Place until he sailed for India on the *Asia* in 1808, for entries in Coutts's ledgers show that Smart was in the habit of giving his son sums of money from time to time, the following amounts being paid to him:

1804	August 23	£20
1805	August 12	50
1805	October 12	20
1807	April 6	20
1807	August 17	10
1807	August 21	10

On 17 August 1808, Smart paid £210 to Captain H. P. Tremenheere as his son's passage money to India, his last recorded payment on the boy's account.[2] Before leaving England, John made a will which was signed at 2 Russell Place, and witnessed by John Stevens. In it he bequeathed all his property to his sister, Sarah, whom he appointed sole executrix. Among the articles retained by Sarah after her brother's death were a number of miniatures and a box of pictures. What became of them is not known, nor do we know who were the sitters portrayed. Smart appears to have taken an adequate amount of equipment with him, including a number of books on art, history, music, and literature, as well as a Bible and Prayer Book, a volume on the *Art of Defence on Foot* and Walpole's *Anecdotes of Painting*. He was well supplied with art materials, paints, sheets of ivory, frames and crystal glasses for covering miniatures, and judging from the list of his effects almost all of these were sold in Madras after his death.

When Sir William Foster wrote on *British Artists in India*[3] he had not been able to trace the name of the ship in which John sailed or when he landed, but it is now known that the ship was the *Asia*, for in the Public Dispatches from England, 1808, a list is given of persons permitted to go to India on the *Asia* and one of those destined for Fort St George was 'Mr John Smart, to practise as a miniature painter'. The ship arrived on 11 February 1809, according to the *Madras Almanac* for the year 1810.

[1] Williamson, *The Miniature Collector*, 1921, pp. 133 and 135.
[2] Messrs Coutts & Co.
[3] *Walpole Society*, Vol. XIX, p. 71.

This is confirmed by a letter to the Chief Secretary to The Government at Fort St George, which is as follows:

To,   11.2.1809
   The Chief Secretary to Government,
      Fort St George.
Sir,
   I have the honour to acquaint you for the information of the Hon' the Governor in Council, of the arrival of the Hon' Company's Ship Asia under my Command . . . having left Portsmouth on 17th September . . .
                              I have the honour to be etc.
                              H. P. TREMENHEERE.
                              Commander of the Asia and senior
                              officer of the Ships in Company.

The other vessels referred to were the *Walthamstow, Ocean,* and *Sir Stephen Lushington,* and the extra ships *Union, General Stuart,* and *Tottenham.*

Soon after his arrival John Smart opened a current account with Harringtons which may well have been his father's bank.

Under 'Madras Intelligence' given in the *Calcutta Monthly Journal* for 12 February 1809, mention is made of the arrival of the *Asia,* and John Smart, Junior's, name appears at the head of a list of nine cadets who had travelled in her. The possibility of his having hoped to obtain a cadetship is not precluded, in spite of the absence of a cadet paper and the fact that the East India Company had granted him permission to go to India as a miniaturist.

From the list of his effects which were sold in Madras, he is known to have had the following equipment with him:

>   1 Spy Glass with Case
>   1 Cocked Hat
>   1 Case Tuning Instrument
>   1 Sword with Belt
>   1 Tambrin with Stick & Tryangle
>   1 Pistol
>   1 Red Coat with an Epaulet
>   1 Flute[1]

His time in Madras was of short duration, for four months after his arrival he died. In spite of exhaustive inquiries nothing has so far been discovered about his life there or the cause of his death. The entry in the Register of Burials at St Mary's Church, Fort St George, gives the date of death as 1 June 1809, although the *Madras Courier* of 7 June records

[1] India Office Records, Commonwealth Relations Office.

it as on 2 June. No monument to his memory appears to have been erected.

His will was proved by his sister, Sarah, on 14 February 1810, before the Worshipful John Daubany, Surrogate, as spinster, sister, and sole executrix. Letters of administration of his estate and effects were granted to Gilbert Ricketts, Esq., Registrar of the Madras Probate Court, on 10 July 1809, and there is a Registrar's certificate showing that on 12 October 1810 an account of the administrators was filed. The total estate, including the money raised by the sale of his personal effects, amounted to 859 pagodas, 33 fanams, 20 cash, of which, after the necessary expenses had been deducted, 381 pagodas, 39 fanams, 3 cash was paid to the Honourable Company's Treasury, together with a box containing pictures, one drawing table containing miniatures, one snuff box, one gold ring, and one medal of John Smart, Senior.[1]

Sarah Smart later executed a power of attorney in favour of John Dighton, husband of Sophia, her half-sister, who had died in 1793, to act as her agent, and to receive the money on her behalf, and on 6 August 1811, Ricketts filed a petition for payment of the balance of the estate to Lieutenant-Colonel John Dighton (as he then was) as Sarah Smart's agent. It is evident from the information now available that in spite of the various changes that took place within it, Smart's family was united and in close contact with each other.

Smart Junior's work as an artist is not comparable with that of his father in artistic merit. In spite of the fact that it closely resembles that of Smart Senior, it has not the quality of draughtsmanship and colouring so unmistakable in the older man's work. The son often placed his sitter rather to the bottom of the picture with a large space above the sitter's head, whereas the father had a greater aptitude for composition. In some cases more than others there is a greater resemblance between the two men's art, and one is inclined to wonder if in these cases he did not have his father's assistance; certainly in some portraits he copied the elder man's work. Basil Long says: 'Those of his miniatures which I have seen were weaker and larger than most of his father's, although showing considerable technical affinity to them.'

The majority of his paintings were on paper or card, although he occasionally used ivory. Some were executed in blacklead, a self-portrait in this medium being exhibited at the Royal Academy in 1808. This may have been the plumbago portrait noted by Basil Long, and photographed by the British Museum in 1942. An engraving of this portrait

[1] Madras Records, C.R.O.

was made by John Smart, Junior, but not as far as is known ever published. The self-portrait is now in the collection of Edward G. Paine of New York. The features do not bear much resemblance to those of his father, and he seems to have been of a slighter build altogether. He used a signature very like that of Smart Senior, 'J. S. J. [Junior]', in cursive script and besides this signed 'J. Smart Jun.' or 'J. Smart Junior'; most of his portraits are dated. A fine example of his work, a portrait of Captain (later Admiral) Robert Williams from the late Mr H. Burton Jones's collection, was illustrated by Basil Long in the *Connoisseur*, April 1926—signed 'John Smart Jun. 1801', it has a seascape background. A miniature of an officer was in the collection of the late C. W. Dyson Perrins and was sold in December 1958. It depicted an officer with short powdered hair and side-whiskers, wearing a scarlet coat with gold epaulettes; the background was grey-brown stippling, and the miniature was set in an oval locket, 2 in. long, with a coil of hair and a monogram, set over an opalescent enamel ground decorating the reverse.

Although a number of miniatures and portrait drawings were sold at Christie's in 1928, the works of John Smart, Junior, are generally scarce and it is not possible to give any sort of list of his sitters as can be done in the case of his father. The following miniatures, however, have been ascribed to him by Algernon Graves, F.S.A., and were exhibited at the Royal Academy.

Year exhibited

1800	686	Mr Edwards.
	906	Mr R. Paine.
1802	542	Miss A. S. Edwards.
	646	Mr Dodgson.
1803	504	Mr Boyd.
	855	Portrait of a young lady.
1808	571	Self-portrait in blacklead.
	785	A frame containing the portraits of Miss Green, Miss M. A. Green, and Miss F. Green.
	827	His Serene Highness the Prince of Conde.

The Green family were related by marriage, the elder sister, Augusta Ann, having married Robert Woolf, eldest son of Anna Maria, who was John Junior's half-sister. The miniature of Miss Mary Anne Green, signed and dated 1807, which was at one time in the Francis Wellesley Collection, was sold at Sotheby's in 1920 and is now at the Victoria and Albert Museum. In it the sitter wears a mauve Empire gown with a lace collar. The whereabouts of the portrait of the third sister, Miss F. Green, is unknown. Another miniature known to exist painted by John Junior, signed and dated 1806 and owned by Mrs Burton Jones, is that of the Hon. Edward P. Lygon, son of Earl Beauchamp. A miniature of Horatio Townshend, Esq., signed and dated 1801, and of the Hon. Mrs Walpole, signed and dated 1806, were sold at Christie's on 3 December 1963.

The oil portrait of Sir Jamsetjee Jejeebhoy (1783–1859) at the Oriental Club, listed by Basil Long as by John Smart, Junior, could not have been his work.

An interesting set of ten pencil drawings after the well-known portraits by Hans Holbein, now at Windsor, came into the sale-rooms on 13 November 1962, and are now in my collection. They are dated 1798 and must have been drawn from the originals, as several of them were not engraved before 1812. They are good strong drawings, and although they have a look of John Smart's modelling about them, are faithful copies of the originals. They include Sir John Godsalve, The Earl of Surrey, one called 'Anne of Cleves', Judge Moore and six others.[1]

In spite of John Smart's hopes of his son's attainments, he did not show signs of rising to anything like the heights of his father in artistic ability, and but for the similarity in style and technique, and the fact that he was Smart's son, it is unlikely that he would have been singled out from the ranks of his contemporaries.

[1] Williamson, *The History of Portrait Miniatures*, Vol. I, p. 7.

APPENDIX A

List of Known Sitters

LIST OF sitters compiled from Private and Public Collections, Sale Catalogues, etc. Every endeavour has been made to discover the whereabouts of portraits, but there will inevitably be many that have not come to my notice, and for these omissions I apologize. It has not been possible to include the numerous miniatures of unknown sitters.

ABBOTT, MR CHARLES

ABERNETHY, MRS., signed and dated 1800

ABINGDON, CHARLOTTE, *née* WARREN, 4TH COUNTESS of, (1) signed in full and dated 1777, (2) dated 1778

ABINGDON, WILLOUGHBY BERTIE, 4TH EARL OF, dated 1768

ABINGDON, LADY, dated 1778

ADAM, DR LAW, dated (1) 1773, (2) 1778

AGUILOR, DR, *c.* 1783

ALEXANDER, COLONEL KEITH MICHAEL, dated 1810

ALEXANDER, GENERAL PATRICK, dated 1795

ALLAN, SIR ALEXANDER, BART., M.P., signed and dated 1787 I

ALLAN, WILLIAM RANKIN, dated 1783

ALSOP, RICHARD, ESQ., signed

ALVES, WILLIAM, *c.* 1801

ANCASTER, DUCHESS OF (after Sir Joshua Reynolds)

ANCASTER, MARY, DUCHESS OF, wife of 3rd Duke, signed and dated 1763

ANCASTER, ROBERT, 4TH EARL OF (1756–79), dated 1775

ANDERSON, MISS E., signed in full and dated 1810

ANDERSON, DR JAMES, *c.* 1794

ANDRAS, MISS

ANKEE, GOVERNOR OF TRANQUEBAR

ANSTRUTHER, SIR ALEXANDER OF THIRD PART (1769–1819), signed and dated 1764

ARCOT, MUHAMMAD ALI, NAWAB WALLAJAH OF, AND PRINCE OF THE CARNATIC (1718–95), (1) dated *c.* 1787—on tinted paper rectangular, (2) dated 1787—on ivory and signed, (3) dated 1788 I, (4) dated 1792 I, and another 1792, (5) dated 1795 I, (6) dated 1797 I, (7) *c.* 1798

ARMSTEAD, MRS

ARMYTAGE, SIR GEORGE, (1) as a child, (2) later

ARNOLD, MR

ARNOTT, CHARLES, ESQ., dated *c.* 1800

ARTHUR, GENERAL SIR GEORGE

ASTON, THE HON. HARRIET HERVEY, dated 1781

AUBIN, JOHN

AUBIN, MRS ST., signed and dated 1785

AUBREY, COLONEL GEORGE WILLIAM, dated 1787 I

AUBREY, MISS, afterwards MRS THOMAS LEWIS COKER

AURIOL, CAPTAIN

AUSTEN, MISS PHILADELPHIA (after Mrs T. S. Hancock, aunt of Jane Austen),
 miniature set in a ring

AWSITER, DR, *c.* 1772

BAILEY, MRS, dated 1776

BAIRD, WILLIAM, ESQ., SENIOR, dated 1767

BAIRD, WILLIAM, ESQ., JUNIOR, dated 1767

BAKER, COLONEL, of 1st Reg. Foot, dated 1783

BAKER, MRS FRANCES, wife of Colonel Baker, dated 1783

BAKER, QUARTERMASTER, of the *Dutton*

BALCHIN, ELIZABETH

BALDWIN, THE HON. MRS, dated 1782

BALLARD, MR, dated 1798

BANKS, MAJOR, of Madras, signed and dated 1789 I

BANTINGS, MR

BARCLAY, ROBERT, of Clapham, signed and dated 1783

BARCLAY, MRS ROBERT (*née* ANNE FORD), signed and dated 1783

BARKER, MISS

BASTARD, EDMUND, ESQ., dated 1766

BATHURST, MISS MARY, dated 1792 I

BATSON, MR

BAYLEY, MR, father-in-law of John James Smart

BEAUCHAMP, COUNTESS, signed and dated 1780 (see DENN)

BECKFORD, PETER, ESQ., dated 1779

BECKFORD, MRS PETER, signed and dated 1782

BECKFORD, MRS WILLIAM, signed

BELLAMONT, EMILY, COUNTESS OF

BENET, MISS

BENNETT, MISS

BERESFORD, THE HON., MRS dated 1779, sister of Marchioness Townshend

BETTY, WILLIAM HENRY WEST (The Young Roscius), signed and dated 1806

BINNEY, CHARLES, 1797, secretary to Nawab of Arcot

BINNEY, MISS, dated 1806, by John Smart Junior ⎫ daughters of

BINNEY, MISS HARRIET, dated 1807, by John Smart Junior ⎭ Charles

BIRD, MR

BLAIR, CAPTAIN

BLAIR, SIR JAMES HUNTER, 1772

BLIGH, CAPTAIN WILLIAM, of the *Bounty* and the *Director*

BOOTH, THE HON. ELIZA (*obiit* 1765), copied 1766 (after portrait by Francis
 Cotes, 1764)

BOOTY, MR, dated 1797

BOSTON, LORD, dated 1777
BOSTON, FREDERICK, 2ND LORD, 1776
BOSTON, CHRISTINA, 2ND LADY, dated *c.* 1780
BOUVERIE, MR
BOUVERIE, MR BERTIE—possibly identical with above
BOYD, HUGH, ESQ., *c.* 1793
BOYD, LIEUTENANT-GENERAL SIR ROBERT, K.B. (1710–94), (2) dated 1784 (two miniatures, one in uniform, one in plain clothes)
BOYD, LADY, previous called wife of Sir Robert, dated 1784 (see CHARLOTTE LEIGHTON)
BOYDELL, MISS MARY
BRAMIN,[1] SINIVERSANT THE, dated 1790
BRAMIN,[2] VACNATARAMMAN THE
BRAWBRIDGE, MRS, *c.* 1781
BRENNEN, MR, Recorder of Cork, signed and dated 1766
BROMLEY, SIR GEORGE, BART., signed and dated 1780
BROMLEY, THE HON. ESTHER (*née* CURZON), wife of Sir George, signed and dated 1782
BROOKE, CHARLES, signed and dated 1796 I
BROOKE, COLONEL ROBERT, Governor of St Helena, dated 1783
BRUCE, JAMES, explorer (1730–94), dated 1776
BRUCE, THE HON. CHARLES ANDREW
BRUMMELL, MRS, signed and dated 1780
BRUNSWICK, THE DUCHESS OF (called), dated 1786 I
BUCHAN, HON. MRS
BUCKINGHAM, HON. MRS
BUCKNELL, MR
BULLOCK, MRS
BURDETT, CAPTAIN
BURELL, CAPTAIN PERCY (1779–1807), dated 1805
BURGESS, CAPTAIN RICHARD, of the *Ardent,* dated 1797
BURKE, WILLIAM, *c.* 1792
BURKE, MRS, dated *c.* 1799
BURR, COLONEL, dated 1799
BURR, MRS, dated 1811
BURR, LIEUTENANT-GENERAL DANIEL, signed and dated 1799
BURR, MAJOR-GENERAL
BURROUGHS, LAETITIA (afterwards LADY OGLE), signed
BURROUGHS, LOUISA (afterwards LADY STRANGE), signed and dated 1797
BURROUGHS, MRS, and her four children (LOUISA, LETITIA, WILLIAM, and MARIA)
BURT, MISS
BUTLER, CAPTAIN JOHN, or TOM
BUXTON, SARAH (m. Charles Dumbleton), dated 1777

CALDWELL, LADY, dated *c.* 1777
CAMPBELL, GENERAL SIR ARCHIBALD, K.C.B. OF INVERNEILL (1739–91), dated 1772

[1,2] Brahman

CAMPBELL, GENERAL SIR ARCHIBALD, K.C.B. (1739–91), (1) sketch, *c.* 1775, (2) dated 1778 I
CAMPBELL, MRS DUGALD (*née* ELIZABETH MACKAY), dated 1787 I
CAMPBELL, SIR JAMES, BART., signed and dated 1786 I
CAMPBELL, MISS (child)
CAPPER, COLONEL, of Bungay, dated 1778
CAPPER, DOROTHY, daughter of Colonel Capper, signed and dated 1778
CAPPER, MISS MARIANNE, dated 1778
CAREW, SIR GARVEN
CAREW, THE HON. REGINALD POLE, signed and dated 1784
CARLISLE, LORD
CARTARET, BARON, signed and dated 1766
CAULFIELD, SIR GEORGE, dated 1779
CHAMBERS, LADY, signed and dated 1792 I
CHAMBERS, MISS, dated 1807
CHAMPION, COLONEL ALEXANDER, signed and dated 1769. C.-in-C. of E.I. Coy.
CHARLES, MR
CHARLTON, WILLIAM OF HERBYARDS
CHARNIER, MRS (*née* GEORGINA GRACE BURNABY), dated 1786
CHASE, MRS
CHASE, THOMAS, signed and dated 1787 I
CHESTERFIELD, PHILIP DORMER, 4TH EARL OF, dated 1764
CLARE, JOHN FITZGIBBON, EARL OF, signed and dated 1767
CLEARMOUNT, MADAM DE
CLEMENTS, JOHN, ESQ., dated 1798
CLERK, ROBERT, 1787 I
CLINTON, GENERAL SIR HENRY, K.B., dated *c.* 1777
CLIVE, LADY, dated 1770
CLIVE, LORD, dated 1778
CLOSE, MAJOR-GENERAL SIR BARRY, BART., dated 1794 I
COBURN, THOMAS, M.C.S., dated 1789 I
COCKAYNE, THE HON. WILLIAM (1756–1809), dated 1782, and sketch *c.* 1782
COCKBURN, THOMAS, 1789
COCKBURN, THOMAS, dated 1790 I
COCKBURN, SIR WILLIAM, BART., dated 1791 I, and 1786
COLBORNE, MR, of Bath
COLLINS, MISS ANNE
COLLINS, MASTER GEORGE, signed and dated 1799
COLLINS, MASTER HENRY JOHN
COLLINS, MISS ROSE
COLQUHOUN, PATRICK, dated 1807/8
COLVILLE, LADY, signed and dated 1788 I
COMYNS, MRS
CONNOR, MARIANNE, daughter of George Connor, of Cork, later wife of 2nd Baron Lisle
CONWAY, MAJOR-GENERAL, Governor of Pondicherry, dated 1792 I
COOK, CAPTAIN, of the 'Blues'
COOPER, MARGARET, of Edinburgh, dated 1778

CORDER, T., ESQ., dated 1769
CORNISH, CAPTAIN
CORNWALLIS, CHARLES, 1ST MARQUIS, (1) dated 1787 I, (2) dated 1792 I, (2a) sketch signed in full and dated 1792, (3) dated 1793 I
CORNWALLIS, LADY (called), signed and dated 1793 I
CORRY, LOUISA MARY ANN, b. 1781 (child)
COSWAY, MARIA (called), signed and dated 1784
COTTINGHAM, MISS ELIZABETH, of County Clare, dated 1777
COTTON, CAPTAIN HENRY, of Crakemarsh and 33rd Foot, (1) *c.* 1764, (2) dated 1765
COURTS, MR
COURTOWN, THE COUNTESS OF
CRAVEN, LORD WILLIAM, dated January 1783
CRAWFORD, HENRY, dated 1786 I
CRUTCHLEY, GEORGE HENRY, dated 1804
CRUTTENDEN, JOHN HOLDEN, d. 1771, signed and dated 1779. After a portrait by Sir Joshua Reynolds
CRUTTENDEN, JOHN HOLDEN, 1756–1832, signed and dated 1779
CUMBERLAND, H.R.H. PRINCE HENRY FREDERICK, DUKE OF (1745–90), Captain H.M.S. *Venus*, (1) dated 1769, (2) dated 1785
CUMBERLAND, ANNE, DUCHESS OF (*née* LUTTRELL) (1753–1803), (1) dated *c.* 1775, (2) sketch
CUNNINGHAM, MR
CUPARS, MRS, dated 1807
CURRAN, RT HON. JOHN PHILPOT, dated 1788
CUSSANS, MRS, dated 1780, and another 1775

DALLAS, MR, dated 1782
DALLING, COLONEL, of Jamaica (afterwards LIEUTENANT-GENERAL SIR JOHN DALLING)
DALRYMPLE, LORD, probably JOHN, 5th Earl of Stair
DAMER MRS ANNE, *née* SEYMOUR CONWAY, afterwards LADY MILTON
DARELL, LADY (*née* MARY BECHER), dated 1779
DARELL, MISS AMELIA, (1) 1784, (2) dated 1785
DAVIDSON, MR ALEXANDER, of Drumhall, signed and dated 1786 I
DAVIDSON, ALEXANDER (of Drumhall, N.B., 1740–91), signed and dated J.S. 1786 I
DAVY, MAY
DAVY, WILLIAM, MAJOR, signed and dated 1775
DAY, SIR JOHN, dated 1777
DAY, MRS
DEAS, MISS CAROLINE
DEAS, JOHN, dated 1773
DEAS, MRS JOHN, 1773
DEBONNAIRE, MISS, dated 1788 I
DEERING, LADY, possibly LADY DEARING
DENHAM, SIR JAMES STEUART, dated 1790
DENN, CATHERINE (later COUNTESS BEAUCHAMP), (1) signed and dated 1779, (2) signed and dated 1780

DENT, LIEUTENANT JOHN, Bengal Infantry, signed and dated 1790 I
DENTON, MISS
DERING, LADY, 2nd wife of Sir Edward Dering, 6th Bart., *née* DEBORAH WIN-
  CHESTER
DEVONSHIRE, THE DUCHESS OF, GEORGIANA
DEVONSHIRE, MARY, MARCHIONESS OF, 2nd wife of 1st Marquis, dated 1777
DICKENSON, MR
DIGHTON, JAMES, ESQ., dated 1790 I
DIGHTON, JAMES LUCY, dated 1790 I
DIGHTON, JOHN (1793–1810), dated 1804
DIGHTON, JOHN, dated 1810
DIGHTON, MAJOR, dated 1791 I
DIGHTON, RICHARD, dated 1791 I
DIGHTON, SOPHIA (*née* Smart), dated 1790, and another, 1788
DILLON, THE VISCOUNTESS
DIXIE, MR
DOBSON, WILLIAM, by John Smart, Junior, sketch, signed and dated 1800
DOGARTY, MR JOHN, dated 1785
DONVILLE, MARIA, signed and dated 1807
DONVILLE, WILLIAM, signed and dated 1807
DOUGHTY, MR
DOUGLAS, CAPTAIN HON. JOHN, 1st Foot Guards, signed and dated 1783
DRAKE, MRS
DRAKE, MARY FRANCES, married 4th Earl of Macclesfield, signed and dated, 1781
DRAKE FAMILY, a gentleman, member of the, signed and dated 1779
DRUMMOND, JOHN, ESQ. (1754–88), dated 1784
DRUMMOND, CAPTAIN PATRICK, Royal Artillery, signed and dated 1791 I
DRURY, CAPTAIN O'BRIEN
DUMBLETON, MR
DUMBLETON, MRS CHARLES (*née* BUXTON), dated 1777
DUNCAN, ADMIRAL, THE RT HON. VISCOUNT, signed in full and dated 1798
DUNLOP, JOHN

EDGEWORTH, RICHARD LOVELL, father of Maria, signed and dated 1780
EDGEWORTH, MISS, probably MARIA
EDMONSTONE, MRS BENJAMIN, dated 1788 I
EGMONT, JOHN JAMES, 3RD EARL OF
ELIZABETH, PRINCESS, daughter of George III (?)
ELLISON, MR S.
ESSINGTON, CAPTAIN WILLIAM H., of the *Triumph*, dated 1797
EXMOUTH, LORD, dated 1798 or 1791 (?)

FANSHAWE, CAPTAIN, R.N.
FANSHAWE, ROBERT, ESQ., R.N., signed and dated 1763 (two miniatures)
FANSHAWE, MRS ROBERT (CHRISTINA) (*née* GENNEYS), signed
FEATHERSTONHAUGH, MR
FENTON, THOMAS, dated 1776
FENTON, MRS
FISHER, MISS

FITZHERBERT, MR
FITZHUGH, MRS
FLOYD, LIEUTENANT-COLONEL, 9th Dragoons, signed and dated 1796, J. Smart, Junior
FLOYD, SIR JOHN, dated 1791
FOLEY, a member of the family, signed and dated 1773.
FOLKES, LADY, dated *c.* 1772
FOULKES, SIR MARTIN
FRANCIS, SIR PHILIP (1740–1818), signed and dated 1781
FRANK, DR RICHARD, dated 1783
FRASER, MRS, signed in full and dated 1776
FRITH, MASTER, dated 1791 I
FRITH, COLONEL ROBERT, signed and dated 1791 I
FRITH, MRS ROBERT, signed and dated 1791 I

GAMBIER, MR
GARNETT, MISS NELLIE, dated 1770
GARROW, MR (afterwards RT HON. SIR WILLIAM GARROW), signed and dated 1788 I
GASCOINE, MISS, dated 1775
GEMELL, MR
GILBERT, ANDREW LYNCH, signed and dated 1766
GODFREY, MR
GOLDENHAM, JOHN, of Madras, dated 1808
GOMONDE, RICHARD MAJOR, of Madras, signed and dated 1790
GOMONDE, MRS (*née* SUSANNAH ELLERKER), signed and dated 1790
GOODRICH, H. G., ESQ., of York
GORING, ELIZABETH, signed and dated 1777
GOSFORD, ARTHUR, IST EARL OF, dated 1773
GOUGH, CHARLOTTE, signed and dated 1770
GOUGH, SIR HARRY (afterwards IST LORD CALTHORPE), dated 1783
GOULBURN, MR
GOULBURN, MISS
GRAHAM, JAMES
GRANT, MRS ELIZABETH (?)
GREEN, MISS, dated *c.* 1808, by John Smart, Junior
GREEN, MISS F., by John Smart, Junior
GREEN, MISS M. A., by John Smart, Junior
GREGORY, COLONEL
GRIER, MISS
GRIMES, ABRAHAM, 1774, signed
GRIMES, MARY, *née* CHOLMLEY, signed and dated 1774
GRIMKE, MR
GRIMS, MRS, or GRIMES
GRIMSTON, MRS
GRUBER, MRS, or GRUCHER
GUILDFORD, 2ND EARL OF, signed and dated 1767

HAKE, THOMAS, of Clapham, dated 1781

HAKE, MARY, wife of Thomas, dated 1781

HALL, MRS, signed and dated *c.* 1785

HAMILTON, ADMIRAL, R.N., dated 1778 (?)

HAMILTON, ADMIRAL CHARLES POWELL, R.N., signed and dated 1777

HAMILTON, CAPTAIN CHARLES POWELL, R.N., dated 1778

HAMILTON, MRS (*née* LUCRETIA PROSSER), wife of Admiral Charles Powell
  Hamilton.

HAMILTON, COLONEL, sketch

HAMILTON, COLONEL JAMES (174(?)–1804), dated *c.* 1784

HAMMOND, MISS, signed and dated 1779

HANSFORD, CAPTAIN

HARCOURT, THE REV. MR

HARE, JAMES (1749–1804), *c.* 1774

HARRIS, MR

HASTINGS, WARREN (1732–1818)

HASTINGS, MRS, wife of Warren Hastings

HAUGHTON, MR

HAUGHTON, MRS (*née* NANCY PARSONS (?), afterwards m. Charles, 6th Lord
  Maynard)

HAWARTH, MRS

HAY, CAPTAIN, of the Guards, dated 1774

HAY, JAMES, 13th EARL OF ERROLL

HAY, MISS (as a child)

HAYES, CAPTAIN, of the *Melville Castle*, dated 1785

HEARNE, THOMAS, dated 1783

HENCHMAN, THOMAS, dated 1785

HENCHMAN, MRS

HENDERSON, JOHN (actor), dated 1780

HENEHUMAN, MRS

HERVEY, CAPTAIN JOHN AUGUSTUS, LORD, R.N., dated 1782

HERVEY, HON. THOMAS, 1st Foot, dated 1764

HERVEY, HON. THOMAS, 1st Foot, dated 1774

HILL, MISS BARBARA, signed and dated 1777, afterwards MRS WILLIAM COCK-
  AYNE

HILL, BRYAN, signed and dated 1770

HOARE, MR

HOBART, LORD ROBERT (afterwards 4TH EARL OF BUCKINGHAMSHIRE),
  dated 1793 I

HOLBECK, MR (?) WILLIAM

HOLLAND, MISS (afterwards MRS CRAWFORD), signed and dated 1799

HOLLAND, MR, signed and dated 1806

HOOD, SIR WILLIAM, dated 1766

HOPE, SIR ARCHIBALD, 9TH BART, dated 1780

HOWE, LORD, signed and dated 1780

HORNE, MR (?), dated 1775

HOWARD, COLONEL (afterwards LORD SURREY)

HOWARTH, MR, or HAWORTH

HOWARTH, MRS

HUGHES, LADY, signed and dated 1800

HURLOCK, MISS ANN, dated 1776
HYNDFORD, THOMAS, 5th Earl of, signed and dated 1764

IBETSON, MR
IMPEY, SIR ELIJAH, signed and dated 1799
IMPEY, MASTER JOHN, 3rd son of Sir Elijah, signed and dated 1785
INCE, MR
INDIAN YOUTH, PRINCE OF THE CARNATIC (?), dated 1788 I
INNES, HUGH, ESQ., signed and dated 1799
INNES, SIR HUGH, of Lochalsh (1704–1801), signed and dated 1799
IRBY, THE HON. MRS, dated 1781
IRBY, THE HON. WILLIAM, dated 1781

JACKSON, MRS MARY, signed 1776
JAMES, MR, dated 1774
JENKINS, JOHN, R.N., dated 178(?)
JERSEY, THE COUNTESS OF, 1784
JODDREL, MR
JOHANNA, GOVERNOR OF, dated 1785
JOHNSON, MR JAMES, of Glasgow, signed and dated 1776
JOHNSON, DR, signed and dated 1808, John Smart, Junior
JOHNSON, DR WILLIAM, surgeon of the *Dutton*, dated 1785
JOHNSTON, LADY CHARLOTTE, signed and dated 1772
JOLLIFFE, WILLIAM, dated 1770 (?)
JOLLIFFE, ELEANOR, wife of William, dated 1774
JOLLIFFE, HILTON, WILLIAM, JOHN AND GEORGE, sons of the above. Group, dated 1791
JOLLIFFE, GEORGE
JONES, MR
JONES, WILLIAM, dated 1764/5
JONES, the landscape painter (?), probably THOMAS

KANNOUGH, THE COUNTESS, signed and dated 1774
KAUFFMAN, ANGELICA, R.A. (called), signed and dated 1764
KEATING, MISS, signed and dated 1811
KEATING, COLONEL HENRY S., dated (1) March 1806, (2) retouched 1807, (3) 1808
KENNETT, RICHARD, signed and dated 1784
KETTLE, MR
KIDD, COLONEL, of Madras, signed and dated 1790 I
KILLMAURS, LORD
KIMPE, MRS
KINGSLEY, MR
KINGSTON, MRS
KIRK, MR JOACHIM, the seal engraver
KNATCHBULL FAMILY, A LADY OF THE, dated *c.* 1778
KNIGHT, SIR J.
KYD, CAPTAIN ALEXANDER, dated 1790

LACEY, MICHAEL ROLPHINO, age 12

LAMBE, CAPTAIN, signed and dated 1795

LAMBERT, THE MISSES, signed and dated 1800

LEIGHTON, CHARLOTTE (Niece of Lady Boyd), signed and dated 1784

LENNOX, MRS CHARLOTTE, dated 1777

LESTER, SIR JOHN (?), dated *c.* 1770

LEWIN, MISS MARY, signed and dated 1776

LEWIN, MRS, signed and dated 1784

LEWIN, THOMAS, 99th Foot, signed and dated 1784

LIEL, LIEUTENANT THOMAS, R.N.

LIGHT, MRS, dated 1777

LIGHT, MRS, sketch

LIND, MRS FRANCIS (daughter of Richard Cooper), signed and dated 1785

LINDSAY, LADY, signed and dated 1787

LINDSAY, HON. HUGH, dated 1799 and 1800

LINDSAY, CAPTAIN, later REAR-ADMIRAL SIR JOHN, K.B., dated 1781

LINDSEY, HON. CAPTAIN

LINTON, LORD (possibly CHARLES STUART, 8TH EARL OF TRAQUAIR), dated 1771

LISLE, LADY MARIANNE, dated 1784 (see CONNOR)

LIVESAY, JOHN, dated 1785

LLOYD, MRS (afterwards MRS BECKFORD), signed and dated 1780

LORAINE, ADMIRAL, R.N., signed and dated 1780

LOWTHER, LADY MARY

LYGON, THE HON. MRS CATHERINE

LYGON, THE HON. EDWARD P., by John Smart, Junior, 1806

MACARTNEY, LADY (enamel)

MACALISTER, GENERAL

MACAULAY, GENERAL COLIN (1760–1836), dated 1792 I

MACCLESFIELD, 4TH EARL OF (?)

MACCLESFIELD, THE COUNTESS OF (*née* MARY FRANCES DRAKE), dated 1781

MACDONALD, LADY

MACKAY, DR

MACKINTOSH, CAPTAIN

MACLANE, MR, of Somerset Street, Portman Square

MACPHERSON, SIR JOHN, signed and dated 1787

MALCOLM, CAPTAIN PULTNEY, of the *Donegal* (later VICE-ADMIRAL SIR PULTNEY, K.C.B.), signed in full and dated 1809

MANNING, CAPTAIN EDWARD

MANSFIELD, EARL OF (see MURRAY)

MAQUER, MR

MAQUER, MRS

MARLOW, EDWARD

MARRIOT, GENERAL, dated 1779

MARRIOT, MRS, dated 1755? or 65

MARRIOT, MR

MAUD, MISS DELIA

MAULE, COLONEL EDWARD, dated 1790

MAXWELL, COLONEL, Watercolour on card (playing a violin)
MAXWELL, COLONEL, dated 1785
MEADOWS, GENERAL, signed and dated 1790 I
MEADOWS, GENERAL SIR WILLIAM, K.B. (1738–1813)
MEE, MR, uncle to Lord Palmerston
MEXBOROUGH, JOHN, 1ST EARL OF, dated 1764
MILLER, SIR THOMAS, LORD GLENLEE, signed and dated 1769
MILLS, JOHN, of Bistern and Lincoln's Inn (1750–1820), dated *c.* 1775
MILLS, WILLIAM, dated 1776, and another *c.* 1780
MILNER, MR (see SIR WILLIAM)
MILNER, MRS R. S.
MILNER, SIR WILLIAM
MAC, MADAME LA, dated 1776
MOLESWORTH, SIR ARSCOTT O., dated 1809
MONCKTON, COLONEL, possibly THE HON. HENRY
MONEY, ROBERT, dated 1800
MONK, MR HENRY, dated 1773
MONSON, THE HON. ELIZABETH, dated 1794 I
MONTAGU, ADMIRAL ROBERT, R.N., dated 1772
MONTALBA, COLONEL, signed and dated 1771
MONTROSE, THE DUCHESS OF, signed and dated 1773
MOORE, MRS PETER (*née* SARAH RICHMOND WEBB), dated *c.* 1783
MORRIS, COLONEL VALENTINE (1725–89), Governor of St Vincent, dated 1765
MORRIS, GOVERNOR, OF PIERCEFIELD
MORTIMER, THE HON. MRS, signed and dated 1789
MORTON, SHOLTO, EARL OF
MORTON, KATHERINE, COUNTESS OF, signed and dated 1769
MORTON, MARY (afterwards 3RD wife of John Smart), dated 1804, another *c.* 1804
MOUNT EDGECUMBE, RICHARD, 2ND EARL, dated 1807–8
MURRAY, CHARLES, Consul in Madras (afterwards LORD KENYONS), dated 1772
MURRAY, DAVID, 2ND EARL OF MANSFIELD
MURRY, MRS

NATTES, MR C. C., dated *c.* 1811
NATTES, MR J. W., dated *c.* 1811
NEALE, J. W., 1ST mate of the *Dutton*, *c.* 1785
NEWPORT, MR (SAMUEL OR BENJAMIN), dated 1808
NOLLEKENS, J., dated 1810
NOLLEKENS, MRS

OAKELEY, SIR CHARLES, BART, GOVERNOR OF MADRAS, dated 1786 I
OAKELEY, LADY (*née* HELENA BEATSON) (1762–1835), dated 1786 I
O'BRIEN, CAPTAIN EDWARD
O'BRYEN, CAPTAIN EDWARD, possibly the same as above
OGLANDER, DR JOHN, dated 1779
OGLANDER, LADY
OGLANDER, MISS
O'NEAL, MR, dated *c.* 1784, and another 1795
ONSLOW, ADMIRAL SIR RICHARD, R.N., signed and dated 1798

ORANGE, THE PRINCESS OF
OUGHTON, SIR ADOLPHUS, K.B. (1720–80), dated 1776

PALMER, SIR JOHN, signed and dated 1770
PALMER, CHARLOTTE GOUGH, wife of Sir John Palmer, dated 1770
PARKER, LADY, dated on reverse 1781
PARKER, MRS, OF BATH, dated 1797
PARKHURST, DR, signed and dated 1765
PARRY, THOMAS
PARTRIDGE, MR
PAULET, LADY KATHERINE (later wife of William Henry, 3rd Earl of Darlington)
PAYNE, RALPH (called), dated 1768
PELHAM, MRS, signed and dated 1764, or 1784 (?)
PELLEW, ADMIRAL SIR EDWARD
PERCIVAL, THE HON. EDWARD, signed and dated 1801 and 1799
PERCIVAL, THE HON. MRS EDWARD, signed and dated 1801
PETERS, MRS
PETRIE, MR WILLIAM (afterwards SIR WILLIAM), dated 1789
PETRIE, MRS WILLIAM
PETRIE, MASTER, dated 1789
PHILLIPS, Captain, of the *Ardent*
PHIPPS, JOHN CONSTANTINE, signed and dated 1770, and 1771
PHIPPS, JOHN CONSTANTINE, (aged 17, son of above), signed and dated 1793 I
PITT, THE HON. LOUISA, signed and dated 1782
PLOMER, MR, dated *c.* 1779, and sketch
PLOWDEN, MISS SOPHIA (child), 1785
PLOWDEN, CAPTAIN RICHARD CHICHELE, 70TH FOOT, (1) dated 1777, (2) sketch,
  c. 1777
POLE, ADMIRAL SIR C., signed and dated 1785
POLE, MISS
PONIATOWSKY, PRINCESS, signed and dated 1767
PORCHER, CATHERINE
PORCHER, MRS CHARLOTTE, dated 1787
PORCHER, JOSIAS DUPRE, signed and dated 1787 I
POWYS, MR (possibly THOMAS, later 2ND BARON LILFORD)
PRINGLE, MRS, dated 1799
PROCTOR, LADY LETITIA BEAUCHAMP
PULTNEY, CAPTAIN, of the *Malcolm*, 1809, signed
PULTNEY, CAPTAIN, of the *Malcolm*, sketch for above, signed in full and dated 1809

RADNOR, ANNE, COUNTESS OF
RADNOR, HARRIET, COUNTESS OF
RADNOR, JACOB, 2ND EARL OF
RAINE, DR, of Madras
RAMSAY, MRS, wife of Allan Ramsay, signed and dated 1789 I
RAMUS, MISS
RANKIN, WILLIAM
RANSOME, CAPTAIN, signed and dated 1777
RAWLEY, MISS

READ, MR
REID, DR, dated 1802
REYNOLDS, COLONEL CHARLES, dated 1810
RICHARDSON, COLONEL JOHN (afterwards Lieutenant General), dated 1794
RICHARDSON, MRS, wife of General Richardson (*née* HARRIET EMMA BURNABY)
RICKETTS, SOPHIA, wife of Poyntz Ricketts, esq., signed and dated 1783
RIDLEY, MR
RIDLEY, SIR MATTHEW WHITE, Bart, signed and dated 1788 I
RIVERS, LORD (called), signed and dated 1782
RIVERS, THE HON. JOHN DOUGLAS PITT, dated 1783
ROBSON, MAJOR, St Helena, signed and dated 1795
ROCHE, MR
ROEBUCK, BENJAMIN, dated 1790 I
RUDDIMAN, MRS
RUDDIMAN, WILLIAM
RUMBOLD, CAPTAIN WILLIAM RICHARD
RUSSELL, MR, *c.* 1780
RUSSELL, MRS, of Powick, dated 1781
RUSSELL, MRS (*née* COX), dated 1781
RUSSELL, MR GEORGE

SAGE, JOSEPH, father of Mrs Arthur Shakespeare, dated 1780
SALISBURY, LADY, signed and dated 1781
SAUNDERS, ADMIRAL SIR CHARLES, K.B., signed and dated (1) 1773, (2) 1778
SAVILE (CHARLES or JOHN), of Methley, signed and dated 1774
SAVILE, JOHN, of Methley, signed and dated 1770
SCOTT, MISS ANNE
SCOTT, LADY MARY
SHAKESPEARE, ARTHUR, M.P., signed and dated 1787
SHAKESPEARE, MR and MRS, *c.* 1783
SHAKESPEARE, MR, dated 1776
SHAKESPEARE, MRS, dated 1777
SHARROCK, MR, dated 1777
SHELLEY, SIR JOHN, 6TH Bart, (1) aged 8, dated 1772, (2) dated 1780
SHERIDAN, RICHARD BRINSLEY, signed and dated 1785
SHIPPEY, MRS, dated 1784
SHIRLEY, SIR FRANCIS, *c.* 1750, signed in full
SIDDONS, MRS
SKEFFINGTON, CAPTAIN W. CHARLES FARRELL-
SKRINE, MR
SLOPER, LIEUTENANT-GENERAL SIR ROBERT, K.B., dated 1787 I
SMART, LIEUTENANT CHARLES KENWORTHY, *c.* 1804
SMART, ELEANOR (afterwards LADY CARTARET), signed and dated 1765
SMART, JOHN, self-portraits, (1) self-portrait in crayons 1762, (2) dated 1783, (3) sketch *c.* 1783 (4) dated 1786, (5) sketch signed and dated 1793, (6) signed and dated 1797, (7) signed and dated 1802. (8) dated 1803, (9) dated 1810
SMART, JOHN, infant son of John Smart, signed and dated 1765
SMART, JOHN, JUNIOR, signed and dated 1808
SMART, JOHN, JUNIOR, self-portrait signed and dated 1808

SMART, JOHN JAMES, signed and dated 1807 and another 1806
SMART, MARY (*née* MORTON), (1) dated 1805, (2) signed and dated 1806, (3) signed and dated 1809
SMITH, MISS, signed and dated 1809
SMYTHE, THE HON. MRS
SNEYD, MR
SOLLY, RICHARD, dated 1797
SOMERS, LORD, dated 1782
SOMERS COCKS, MRS THOMAS, signed and dated 1767
SPEDWAY, CAPTAIN, dated 1790 I
STANHOPE, PHILIP, son of 4th Earl of Chesterfield
STEAD, MR, of Tower Hill
STEWART, MR, (1) to the right dated 1777, (2) to the left dated 1777
STEWART, MRS
STOCK, JOHN (age 35), signed and dated 1780
STRANGE, JAMES CHARLES, M.C.S., dated 1789 I
STRANGE, MRS JAMES CHARLES (*née* MARGARET DURHAM), dated 1787 I
STRANGE, LADY (*née* JANET ANSTRUTHER), signed and dated 1783
STUART, CHARLES, 7TH EARL OF TRAQUAIR, signed and dated 1773
STUART, LADY LUCY, signed and dated 1773
SULLIVAN, RICHARD JOSEPH (1ST BARON SULLIVAN) (1752–1806)
SULLIVAN, MRS RICHARD, *c.* 1778
SUMNER, MR
SUTTON, LADY GEORGE (*née* MARY PEART)
SUTTON, JOHN, *c.* 1794
SUWELL, MR
SYDENHAM, MAJOR-GENERAL WILLIAM (1752–1801)
SYKES, MASTER
SYKES, MASTER FRANCIS
STUART, LADY LUCY, signed and dated 1773
ST JOHN, THE HON. JOHN, signed 1770

TADMAN, MISS MARY, signed and dated 1809
TALBOT, LADY CHARLOTTE HILL, COUNTESS, dated 1779–80
TATHWELL, MISS
TAYLOR, MR JAMES, dated 1787
TAYLOR, MRS JAMES, signed and dated 1804
TEIGNMOUTH, LADY CHARLOTTE, wife of Governor-General of India
THANET, MARY, COUNTESS OF, wife of 8th Earl
THURLOW, LORD, dated 1773
TIPU or TIPOO, ABDUL KHALICK SULTAN, SON OF, dated 1794
TIPU or TIPOO, MOOIZ UD DIN SULTAN, SON OF, dated 1794
TOMKINSON, MR, *c.* 1783
TONYN, CAPTAIN ANTHONY, R.N., dated *c.* 1767
TOPPING, MICHAEL (inscribed Madras), *c.* 1795
TOWNDSEND, MRS
TOWNSEND, ELIZABETH, (1) as a girl, (2) older
TOWNSEND, GORE, dated 1767
TOWNSEND, MR

TOWNSEND, MRS SAMUEL, signed and dated 1772
TOWNSHEND, ANNE, MARCHIONESS, signed and dated 1775
TOWNSHEND, ELIZABETH TRELAWNEY
TOWNSHEND, HORATIO, of Bridgemount, Co. Cork, signed and dated 1801,
  John Smart, Junior
TOWNSHEND, MISS
TOWNSHEND, MRS ELIZABETH
TOWRY, CAPTAIN G. N., R.N., signed
TRAVERS, MISS (called), signed and dated 1803
TREVOR, THE HON. MR (possibly JOHN TREVOR HAMPDEN)
TROLLOPE, CAPTAIN HENRY, of the *Russell* (afterwards ADMIRAL SIR HENRY),
  (1) as a captain, (2) as an admiral
TRUSTON, THOMAS, signed and dated 1794 I
TURING, MISS, *c.* 1806
TURING, MISS FRANCES, *c.* 1803
TURNER, MRS DOROTHY, dated 1806
TURNING, MRS, dated 1810
TWINING, MISS, dated 1801
TWINING, MRS
TWINING, THOMAS
TWISDEN, SIR ROGER
TYNTE, COLONEL JOHN KEMEYS-, 1ST FOOT GUARDS
TYNTE, MRS KEMEYS- (*née* JANE HASSELL), *c.* 1765
TYSSEN, SAMUEL (1740–1800), dated 1781
TYSSEN, SARAH (*née* BODICOATE), dated 1781

VERNON, LADY CONSTANCE, signed and dated 1793
VIAPRE, MONSIEUR de

WALES, H.R.H. GEORGE, PRINCE OF, dated 1783 (afterwards GEORGE IV)
WALKER, CAPTAIN, of the *Monmouth*, dated 1798
WALKER, CHARLOTTE, signed and dated 1786 I
WALMESLEY, CAPTAIN JOHN, dated 1779
WALPOLE, THE HON. THOMAS
WALPOLE, THE HON. MRS, dated 1806
WALPOLE, THE HON. MRS, signed and dated 1803, John Smart, Junior
WARD, MR, signed and dated 1769
WARD, MRS (*née* THOMAS)
WARD, MRS HENRY TOWNLEY (*née* ELEANOR HUCKS) (?)
WARNE, LIEUTENANT-COLONEL ROGER, signed and dated 1805
WARNER, MISS, dated *c.* 1779
WARWICK, LORD
WATERFORD, GEORGE DE LA POER, 2ND EARL AND 1ST MARQUIS, dated 1774
WATSON, COLONEL, a sketch
WATSON, COLONEL (1737–86), dated 1786 I
WAY, MISS ABIGAIL, signed and dated 1769. 1st wife of 1st Earl of Sheffield
WEBB, SIR JOHN, signed and dated 1779
WEDDELL, MRS
WELLS, ADMIRAL JOHN, dated 1808

WELLS, CAPTAIN, of the *Dutton*, dated 1785
WELLS, CAPTAIN, of the *Lancaster*
WELLS, CAPTAIN, of the *Monmouth*, dated 1798
WEST, CAPTAIN, of the *Dutton*
WHATMAN, JAMES, dated May 1778 and 1779
WHEATLEY, MR, dated 1780
WHEELER, MRS EDWARD (*née* HARRIET CHICHELE PLOWDEN, 1740–84)
WHITE, MR
WHITE, MRS, dated 1800
WHITE, THOMAS HOLT-, dated 1802
WIGRAM, family group
WIGRAM, SIR ROBERT, 1ST BARONET OF WEXFORD (drawing—oval 4½ in. high), signed and dated 1805
WIGRAM, ROBERT, later 2ND BARONET, son of 1st Baronet of Wexford (assumed name of Fitzwygram) (drawing—oval 4½in. high) dated 1805
WIGRAM, WILLIAM AND JOHN, sons of Sir Robert (drawing—rectangular 7in. high)
WIGRAM, CATHERINE, daughter of Sir Robert (watercolour—oval 4½in. high)
WIGRAM, MARIA, daughter of Sir Robert (pencil and colour—oval 4½in. high)
WIGRAM, SIR ROBERT, and the 2nd Lady Wigram, with Maria, daughter by his first wife and their son William Pitt (heads heightened with colour—oblong 7¾in. wide)
WIGRAM, HENRY AND MONEY, sons of Sir Robert (drawing—oblong 8in. wide)
WIGRAM, HARRIET, ELEANOR AND ANN, daughters of Sir Robert (drawing—oblong 8¾in. wide)
WIGRAM, CHARLES, OCTAVIUS AND JAMES, sons of Sir Robert (drawing—oblong 8½ in. wide)
WIGRAM, JOSEPH, RICHARD, ELY, LOFTUS AND EDWARD, children of Sir Robert and the 2nd Lady Wigram (drawing—oblong 8½ in. wide)
WIGRAM, GEORGE VICESSIMUS, son of Sir Robert (drawing—rectangular 4½ in. high)
WIGRAM, THE SECOND LADY and her son WILLIAM PITT (drawing—rectangular 6½ in. high)
WIGRAMS, MISS
WILKINSON, MR JOHN, dated 1785
WILKS, MRS, of Madras
WILLIAMS, CAPTAIN ROBERT (afterwards ADMIRAL), signed and dated 1801, John Smart, Junior
WILLIAMSON, CAPTAIN
WINCH, MR GEORGE, dated 1784
WINCH, MRS GEORGE, dated 1784
WINGFIELD, COLONEL JOHN, dated 1803
WINGFIELD, HON. MRS, dated 1803
WINSTANLEY, COLONEL, dated 1780
WITHERBRO, MR, Hall Place, Basingstoke, Hants, signed
WOMBWELL, MR
WOOLF, ANNA MARIA (*née* SMART), dated 1788, 1789 I and 1792
WOOLF, ANNA SOPHIA, daughter of Robert and Anna Maria
WOOLF, MISS C.
WOOLF, ELIZABETH ANN, daughter of Robert and Anna Maria
WOOLF, MARIA, daughter of Robert and Anna Maria, dated *c.* 1796

WOOLF, ROBERT, husband of Anna Maria, dated 1786 and 1792
WOOLF, MASTER ROBERT, grandson of John Smart, signed and dated 16 July 1796
WYNCH, JOHN, signed and dated 1784

YATES, THE REV. DR, dated 1762
YATES, MRS, dated 1761
YEATES, JUDGE JASPER (1745–1817)
YOUNG, ADMIRAL, by John Smart, Junior
YOUNG, SIR G.
YOUNG, SIR SAMUEL, 1ST BART, (1) dated 1788 I, (2) dated 1796
YOUNG, EMILY, LADY, dated 1796

Christie's Catalogue

ON THURSDAY, DECEMBER 17, 1936
at one o'clock precisely
Sketches and Studies for Miniature Portraits
by John Smart, the Property of
MRS BUSTEED
Great-granddaughter of the Artist

1 Portrait of Jacob, 2nd Earl of Radnor (1750–1828), three-quarter face to the left, in grey coat; Portrait of his Wife, Anne, daughter and heir of Anthony Duncombe, Lord Feversham of Downton; and Portrait of his mother, Harriet, daughter of Sir Mark Stuart Pleydell, Bart., of Coles Hill, nearly profile to the right—(three)   3

2 Portrait of Lord Dalrymple, probably John, later 5th Earl of Stair, in green coat

3 Portrait of Captain Hay, probably Alexander Leith Hay (1758–1838), in scarlet military coat; Portrait of Colonel Campbell, later Sir Archibald Campbell, K.C.B. (1739–1791), Governor of Madras, 1786; and Portrait of Mr Maclane, of Somerset Street, Portman Square, in grey coat—(three)   3

4 Portrait of Mr Johnson, of Glasgow; Portrait of Captain Skeffington, in scarlet military coat; and Portrait of Captain Cornish—(three)   3

5 Portrait of Lord Killmaurs, probably James Cuninghame, 14th Earl of Glencairn (1749–1791); and Three other Portraits of Unknown Gentlemen—(four)   4

6 Portrait of the Hon. William Cockayne (1756–1809), younger son of Charles, 5th Viscount Cullen, three-quarter face to the left in dove-grey coat
   This is undoubtedly the sketch for the finished miniature Lot 50, in this Catalogue

7 Portrait of a Gentleman, three-quarter face to the left; and Two other Portraits of Gentlemen—(three)   3

8 Portrait of Mr Charlton, in puce coat; Portrait of a Gentleman, in grey coat; and Two Heads of Gentlemen—(four)   4

9 Portrait of Mr Goulburn; and Six other Portraits of Gentlemen—(seven)   7

10 Portrait of Mr Shakespeare, probably Arthur Shakespeare, Esq., M.P.; and Six other Portraits of Gentlemen—(seven)   7

11 Portrait of Mr Hare, of Wimpole Street, in mauve coat; Portrait of Mr Arnold; and Portrait of Mr William Petrie, probably afterwards Sir William Petrie—dated 1789 on the reverse—(three) 3

12 Portraits of Mr Bantings; Portrait of Mr Edgeworth; and Two other Portraits of Gentlemen—(four) 4

13 Portrait of Mr James, in scarlet military coat

14 Portrait of Mr Kingsley, in magenta coat; Portrait of Mr Milner; and Portrait of Mr Sharrock—(three) 3

15 Portrait of Lord Carlisle, of St James's Place, probably Frederick, 5th Earl of Carlisle (1748–1825); and Portrait of a Young Gentleman—(two) 2

16 Head of Judge Jasper Yeates (1745–1817); Head of Mr Wombwell; Head of Mr Dickenson; and Head of a Gentleman—(four) 4

17 Portrait of Mr Sumner; Portrait of Mr S. Ellison; and Portrait of a Gentlemen—(three) 3

18 Portrait of Sir Adolphus (H) Oughton, K.B. (1720–1780), married Mary, widow of John Dalrymple, third son of the 1st Baronet, in scarlet military uniform with blue facings

19 Head of Siniversant the Bramin (1790), and two Portraits of Gentlemen—(three) 3

20 Portrait of H. G. Goodrich, Esq., of York; Head of Colonel Edr Maule—dated 1790; and Head of a Gentleman—(three) 3

21 Head of Lady Folkes; Portrait of Miss Campbell as a child; and Head of a Lady—(three) 3

22 Portrait of Miss Gascoine, in white décolleté and yellow cape, trimmed with fur

23 Portrait of Lady Parker, possibly Bridget, daughter of William Cresswell, of Northumberland, and wife of Sir Harry Parker, 6th Baronet, three-quarter face to the right in green décolleté dress—dated 1781 on the reverse

24 Portrait of Lady Mary Scot, in ermine-trimmed blue cloak; and Portrait of Lady Mary Lowther—(two) 2

25 Portrait of Mrs Dunbleton, *née* Buxton; Head of Mrs Ruddiman; Head of Mrs Bullock; and Head of a Lady—(four) 4

26 Portrait of Mrs Hawarth, with an inscription on the reverse; Portrait of a Lady, in blue dress; and Portrait of a Lady, with long flowing hair, with a bunch of flowers at her bosom—(three) 3

27 Head of Mrs Ward, *née* Thomas, died Aug. 24th, 1800; Head of a Lady; and Head of a Child—(three) 3

28 Portrait of a Lady, in green dress; and Three other Heads of ladies—(four) 4

29 Portrait of a Lady, in blue décolleté frilled dress, and feathers in her hair

30 Portrait of a lady, in pink and blue dress; and Three other Portraits of Ladies—(four) 4

31 Portrait of a Lady, in green dress; Portrait of a Lady, seated, playing a guitar; and Three other Portraits of Ladies—(five) 5

32 Portrait of a Lady, in décolléte and mob cap; and Portrait of a Lady, half-length, in fancy costume—(two) 2

33 Portrait of Captain Phillips, of the 'Ardent', half-length, in uniform

34 Head of Captain Bligh, of the 'Director'

35 Portrait of Captain Burges, of the 'Ardent', in uniform—dated 1797

36 Portrait of Captain Essington, of the 'Triumph', in uniform, later Admiral Essington, of Nottingham Place—dated 1797

37 Head of Sir Henry Trollop, probably Admiral Sir Henry Trollop (1756–1839); Portrait of H. Innes, Esq.—signed and dated, 1799; and Portrait of a Gentleman —pencil—(three) 3

38 Portrait of Master Impey, third son of Sir Elijah Impey, Chief Justice of Bengal inscribed '. . . drawn on board the Dutton Indiaman going to Madras'—dated 1785; and Portrait of Mr Wilkinson, three-quarter length, holding a book, probably Tate Wilkinson (1739–1803), actor and manager of various Yorkshire theatres, published his memoirs in 1790—pencil, heightened with wash—(two) 2

39 Portrait of an Officer, in scarlet coat with yellow facings, and glengarry, with tartan ribbon

40 Portrait of Mr Townsend; and Portrait of Colonel Henry S. Keating. in dark coat and white cravat, the reverse inscribed '. . . 56th Regiment, painted by John Smart in March 1806. No. 2 Russell Place, Fitzroy Sq., retouched from the life in Feby. 1807'—(two) 2
    The 56th Regiment of Foot is now the 2nd Battalion, the Essex Regiment

41 Portrait of a Gentleman, inscribed 'John Smart delint Septr 1795 on board the Melville Castle East Indiaman'—the artist's initials appear on the left-hand bottom corner of the card; Portrait of Michael Topping, Esq., inscribed 'Madras'; Portrait of the Hon. Mr Percival, of Grantham—signed in full, and dated 1801; and Portrait of John Goldenham, Esq., of Madras—signed with initials, and dated 1808—pencil —ovals—(four) 4

42 Portrait of Miss Keating, the reverse inscribed 'Miss Keating, daughter of Michael Keating, Esq., of Madras'—doubly signed with initials and in full, dated 1811; Portrait of Miss Chambers—dated 1807; Head of Sophia Dighton—oval—pencil; Portrait of Miss E. Anderson—signed in full, and dated May 1810; and Portrait of a Lady—pencils and wash—(five) 5

43 Portrait of Captain Hayes, of the 'Melville Castle', in scarlet coat, seated drinking— dated 1785; Portrait of a Naval Officer in uniform; Studies of Hands—signed with initials, and dated 1793; a Study for a Head, the reverse inscribed 'Melville Castle'— red chalk; Head of a Gentleman; and Four Prints, after portraits by John Smart— (nine) 9

44 A Frame, containing a collection of sixteen portraits in pencil, many signed and dated, including the Burroughs Family, a composition of Mrs Burroughs with her

four children—Louisa, Letitia, William and Maria; the Collins children, Master Henry John and Master George Collins; Miss Rose, etc.—mainly ovals

45 Portrait of Mrs Towndsend, three-quarter face to the left, in white dress—in octagonal glazed shagreen case

46 Portrait of the Artist's Second Wife, Mary (died 1853), three-quarter face to the right, in white Empire dress, wearing a pearl necklace—signed, and dated 1809— in oval gold frame, the reverse set with a lock of plaited hair and the monogram 'M.S.'

PICTURE
John Smart

47 Portrait of the Artist, in red Cloak and green vest, sketching—oils
   30¾ in. by 25¼ in.

Christie's Catalogue

ON MONDAY, FEBRUARY 15, 1937

at one o'clock precisely

Sketches and Studies for Miniature Portraits
by John Smart, the Property of

W. H. BOSE, ESQ.

Great-Grandson of the Artist

1 Portrait of Mr Courts, very probably the jeweller to whom so many of Smart's miniatures were sent to be framed; Portrait of Mr Kettle; Head of Mr Mackay; and Four other Sketches of Heads—(seven)   7

2 Portrait of Sir Martin Folkes; Portrait of the Rev. Mr Harcourt; Portrait of Mr Marriot; Portrait of a Gentleman; and Head of a Gentleman—(five)   5

3 Portrait of Colonel Dalling of Jamaica, Portrait of Sir William Milner; and Two other Portraits of Gentlemen—(four)   4

4 Portrait of Mr Cunningham; Portrait of Mr Liel; Portrait of Mr Abbott; and Portrait of a Gentleman—(four)   4

5 Portrait of Mr Holbeck, of George Street, Hanover Square, possibly William Holbeck, Esq., of Mollinton, Farnborough and Radston; Portrait of Mr White; Portrait of Dr Raine, of Madras; and Portrait of Captain Tonyn, in naval uniform —(four)   4

6 Portrait of 'Jones the Landskip Painter'; probably Thomas Jones, born in London about 1730; Head of 'Mr Kirk, the seal engraver', probably John Kirk (1724?– 1788?), medallist and member of the Incorporated Society of Artists; Portrait of a Gentleman in blue coat; and Portrait of an Officer, in scarlet coat with yellow facings —(four)   4

7 Portrait of Mr Powys, possibly Thomas, later 2nd Baron Lilford; Portrait of Captain Fanshawe, of the Navy; Portrait of Mr George Russell, in pink coat; and Head of a Gentleman—(four)   4

8 Portrait of Mr Joddrel; Portrait of Mr Bouverie; Portrait of a Gentleman; and Head of Captain Blair 1—(four)   4

9 Portrait of John Day, Esq., in blue coat; and Portrait of Mr Monk, in grey coat with gold facings—(two)   2

10 Portrait of Lord Linton, probably Charles Stuart, later 8th and last Earl of Traquair, in green coat and pink vest; and Head of the Hon, Mr Trevor, possibly the Hon. John Trevor-Hampden (1749–1824), later 3rd and last Viscount Hampden of the 1776 creation—(two)   2

11 Portrait of Mr Ridley, in mauve coat; Portrait of Mr Gemell; Portrait of Mr Harris; and Head of a Gentleman—(four)   4

12 Portrait of Mr Dixie, three-quarter face to the right, in buff coat

13 Portrait of Mr Stewart, three-quarter face to the right, in grey coat and blue vest

14 Portrait of Mr Stewart, three-quarter face to the left, in grey coat

15 Portrait of Gentleman, nearly full face, in blue coat with white facings, wearing the Ribbon and Order of the Garter

16 Portrait of Gentleman, three-quarter face to the left, in blue coat, white vest and cravat—signed with initials, and dated 1785

17 Portrait of Gentleman, profile to the right; Head of a Brahmin, similar; Portrait of a Girl, similar—pencils and wash; and Five Prints after Portraits, by R. Bowyer and J. Smart—(eight)   8

18 Portrait of Miss Denton; Head of a Lady; and Six other Portraits and Heads of Ladies—(eight)   8

19 Head of Miss Wigrams, of White Lyon Court, Cornhill; and Six other Heads of Ladies—(seven)   7

20 Head of Mrs Gruber; Portrait of a Lady, in blue dress; Portrait of a Lady, in blue coat, trimmed with fur; and Two other Portraits of Ladies—(five)   5

21 Head of Miss Oglander, 'sister to Sir John Oglander of the Isle of Wight'; Head of Miss Pole; and Three other Heads of Ladies—(five)   5

22 Portrait of Mrs Kingston, of Queen's Square, Ormond Street; Head of Mrs Grims; Head of an Old Lady; and Two other Heads of Ladies—(five)   5

23 Portrait of Miss Goulburn; Portrait of a Lady; and Two Heads of Ladies—(four) 4

24 Portrait of Miss Fisher; Portrait of Mrs Grimston; Portrait of a Lady; and Head of a Lady—(four)   4

25 Portrait of the Duchess of Ancaster, in blue dress, seated, leaning her right arm on a balustrade, after the picture by Sir Joshua Reynolds, P.R.A.; and Two other Portraits of Ladies—(three)   3

26 Head of Miss Warner, of Hatton Garden; Portrait of Lady, in blue-white décolleté dress; and Portrait of a Lady, in pink jacket and green turban—(three)   3

27 Portrait of Mrs Armstead, in flowered muslin dress; and Head of a Lady—(two) 2

28 Portrait of a Lady, three-quarter face to the left, in blue-white dress and orange sash

29 Portrait of a Lady, nearly full face, in white dress and mauve tippet, trimmed with fur

30 Portrait of Mrs Light, three-quarter face to right, in grey-white dress; the reverse inscribed: 'Gone to the East Indies Jany 1777'

31 Portrait of Mrs Stewart, three-quarter face to the right, in mauve dress with blue sleeves

32 Portrait of Mrs Hamilton, three-quarter face to the right, in grey-white dress

33 Portrait of Lady George Sutton, probably Mary, daughter of Joshua Peart, Esq., married in 1768, as his second wife, Lord George Manners-Sutton, third son of the 3rd Duke of Rutland, who assumed the latter surname on inheriting the estates of his maternal grandfather, Robert Sutton, Baron Lexington, in 1762, three-quarter face to the left, in pink dress trimmed with green ribbon

34 Portrait of Lady Beauchamp-Proctor; Letitia, eldest daughter and co-heir of Henry Johnstone of Great Berkhampstead, Herts, married, as his second wife, in 1762 Sir William Beauchamp-Proctor, 1st Baronet, three-quarter face to the right, in blue-white dress with ribbons in her hair

35 Portrait of Miss Grier, profile to the right, in riding costume—pencil and wash

36 Portrait of Mrs Fraser, half-length to the left in white dress and blue sash—signed in full; and Portrait of a Lady, half-length, nearly full face—pencil, ovals—(two) 2

37 Portrait of Hugh Boyd, Esq. (1746–1794), Master Intendant of Madras, Secretary to Lord Macartney; Head of the Hon. Capt. Lindsey; and Head of a Lady—(three) 3

38 Portrait of General Meadows, in scarlet military coat with gold facings and white vest—signed with initials, and dated 1790 I; and Portrait of a Gentleman, half-length in bright blue coat and vest, white cravat and ruffles, holding a glass of punch in his left hand—signed with initials, and dated 1774—(two) 2

39 Portrait of Captain Pultney Malcolm (1768–1838) of the 'Donegal', later Vice-Admiral Sir Pultney Malcolm, K.C.B., Commander-in-Chief of the St Helena Station, 1816–17; and later the Mediterranean; in naval uniform—signed in full and dated 1809; and Portrait of Major-General Conway, Governor of Pondicherry, 1792—pencils, ovals—(two) 2

40 Portrait of Major Deighton, half-length to the right, in uniform—signed with initials, and dated 1791 I; and Portrait of James Deighton, Esq., nearly full face, in dark coat and frilled white cravat—signed with initials, and dated 1790 I—pencils—ovals—(two) 2

41 Portrait of Captain Wells of the 'Lancaster'; and Head of Captain Wells of the 'Monmouth'—the reverse inscribed 'Capt. Walker, H.M.S. Monmouth 1798'—(two) 2

42 Portrait of Charles Arnott, Esq., three-quarter face to the right

43 Portrait of Sir John Macpherson (1745–1821), 1st Baronet, Governor-General of India 1785–86, three-quarter face to the left in blue coat—signed with initials, and dated 1787 at Madras, the reverse inscribed 'a sketch of Sir John Macpherson painted at Madras, 1787, on his passage from Bengal to England by Jno Smart'

44 Portrait of Colonel Henry S. Keating, of the 56th Regiment, three-quarter face to the right, in scarlet military coat with blue and white facings—signed with initials and dated 1808 and the reverse signed in full

The 56th Regiment of Foot is now the 2nd Battalion the Essex Regiment

45 Portrait of Mr Dogarty and Dr Johnson, Mr Dogarty in scarlet military coat with green facings, nearly profile to the left, conversing with Dr Johnson, full face, in grey coat and white vest—pencil and wash

46 Portrait of a Gentleman, half-length profile to the right, in dark coat, inscribed 'Jno Smart delint, 1795 on board the Melville Castle, East Indiaman'—pencil—oval

47 Portrait of Lord Hobart (1760–1816); Robert, eldest son of George, 3rd Earl of Buckinghamshire; Governor of Madras 1793–98, and holder of many Government offices, three-quarter face to the right, in dark coat—inscribed 'drawn from recollection at Madras' and dated 1793—pencil—oval

Christie's Catalogue

ON FRIDAY, NOVEMBER 26, 1937
at one o'clock Precisely
Sketches and Studies for Miniature Portraits by
JOHN SMART
(being the third and final portion inherited
from the Artist's Collection)
the Property of
MRS DYER
Great-granddaughter of the Artist

1 Portrait of Mr Skrine, in mauve coat; Portrait of Mr Murray; and Five other Portraits of Gentlemen—(seven)   7

2 Portrait of Colonel Mockton; and Four other Portraits of Gentlemen—(five)   5

3 Portrait of Capt. Plowden, in scarlet military coat with dark facings; and Three other Portraits of Gentlemen—(four)   4

4 Portrait of Mr Mills, of Lincoln's Inn, in mauve coat and green vest; and Three other Portraits of Gentlemen—(four)   4

5 Portrait of Colonel Howard, 'now Lord Surrey', in scarlet military coat with blue facings; and Three other Portraits of Gentlemen—(four)   4

6 Portrait of Mr Partridge, of Clifford Street; Portrait of Mr Colborne, of Bath; and Three other Portraits of Gentlemen—(four)   4

7 Portrait of Mr Dumbleton, in grey-green coat; Portrait of Mr Godfrey, of Lincoln's Inn Fields; Portrait of Mr Grimke; and Head of a Gentleman—(four)   4

8 Portrait of Mr Ibetson; Portrait of Mr Bird; Portrait of Mr Fenton; and Portrait of Mr Howarth—(four)   4

9 Portrait of Lord Egmont, probably John James, 3rd Earl of Egmont (1738–1822); Portrait of Lord Warwick, probably George, 2nd Earl of Warwick (1746–1816); and Portrait of a Gentleman—(three)   3

10 Portrait of Captain Burdett, of the 4th Regiment of Horse, in scarlet military coat with dark facings; and Portrait of Mr Dallas, of Jamaica, in grey coat—(two)   2

11 Portrait of Mr Suwell, in grey coat; and Portrait of a Cleric, in dark coat and frilled cravat—(two)   2

12 Portrait of Colonel Hamilton, No. 3 Leicester Street, Leicester Fields; and Portrait of Mr O'Neal—(two)   2

13 Portrait of Capt. Hamilton; Portrait of Mr Doughty; and Portrait of Mr Bucknell—(three)   3

14 Portrait of Vancataramman Bramin; and Portrait of The Governor of Johanna, an Arabian—dated 1785—(two)   2

15 Portrait of a Gentleman, in green coat, red vest and frilled white cravat, wearing the Star of the Bath—signed with initials, and dated 1788

16 Portrait of Mr Wheatley, in brown coat edged with gold, striped green vest and frilled white stock

17 Portrait of Mr Bertie Bouverie, in grey coat
      Probably Bartholomew (1753–1835), third son of William, 1st Earl of Radnor, by his second wife, Rebecca, second daughter of John Alleyne, of Barbados

18 Portrait of Mr Rumbold, in scarlet military uniform with gold facings

19 Portrait of Captain Cook, of the Blues, in blue coat with scarlet facings and white stock

20 Portrait of Mr Shakespeare, a West Indian, in green coat

21 Portrait of Mr Russell, in grey coat and frilled cravat

22 Portrait of Sir Matthew White Ridley, in pink coat, yellow vest and white cravat
      Sir Matthew White Ridley (1745–1813), 2nd Baronet, M.P., son of Matthew Ridley and Elizabeth, sister of Sir Matthew White, Bart, succeeded his uncle in 1763

23 Portrait of Sir Harry Gough, in grey coat—the reverse dated 18 April, 1783.
      Probably Sir Henry Gough (1749–1798), 2nd Baronet, who assumed the surname of Calthorpe on inheriting, in 1788, the Elvetham and Norfolk Estates from his maternal uncle, Sir Henry Calthorpe, K.B.; raised to the Peerage as 1st Baron Calthorpe in 1796

24 Portrait of George, Prince of Wales, afterwards George IV, in grey coat with frilled cravat wearing the Star of the Garter

25 Portrait of a Lady, half-length, in yellow dress—after Van Dyke; and Eight other Portraits of Ladies—(nine)   9

26 Portrait of Mrs Drake, of Bedford Square; Portrait of Mrs Murray, of Madeira; and Two other Portraits of Ladies—(four)   4

27 Portrait of Mrs Wheler, New Court, Swithin's Lane; and Three other Portraits of Ladies—(four)   4

28 Portrait of Mrs Fitzhugh, in yellow dress with blue riband; and Three other Portraits of Ladies—(four)   4

29 Portrait of Mrs Weddell, in blue dress; Portrait of Mrs Henehuman, in violet dress; and Portrait of a Lady; in blue dress—(three)   3

30 Portrait of Mrs Brawbridge, in grey dress and turban headdress; and Portrait of a Lady, similar—(two)   2

31 Portrait of Mrs Cupars; and Portrait of Mrs Kimpe—(two)   2

32 Portrait of Mrs Day, in grey dress; and Portrait of a Lady, in grey dress trimmed with ermine—(two)   2

33 Head of the Duchess of Devonshire, Georgiana, daughter of John, 1st Earl Spencer, married as his first wife William, 5th Duke of Devonshire, K.G.

34 Head of Mrs Siddons (1755–1831), eldest child of Roger Kemble, Esq., married her fellow actor William Siddons

35 Portrait of Mrs Damer, in grey dress and turban headdress
   Probably Anne Seymour, daughter of Field-Marshal Henry Seymour Conway, married in 1767 the Hon. John Dawson Damer, eldest son of Lord Milton, later Earl of Dorchester

36 Portrait of Mrs Marriot, in mauve dress—dated 1755 on the reverse

37 Portrait of Miss Barker, of Newman Street, in white dress with blue ermine-trimmed jacket and sash

38 Portrait of Lady Salisbury in grey dress and jacket trimmed with fur
   Emily Mary, daughter of Wills, 1st Marquess of Devonshire, married James, 1st Marquess of Salisbury, K.G., F.R.S.; she was burnt to death in the fire at Hatfield, 27th November 1835

39 Portrait of Mrs Beresford, 'Lady Townsend's sister'—possibly Miss Mainwaring-Ellerker, of Risby Park, Co. York—in mauve dress—dated Jany 1779 on the reverse; and Three other Portraits of Ladies—(four)   4

40 Portrait of Mrs Wilks, of Madras, in feathered hat—signed with initials, and dated 1793; Head of a Lady; and Studies for the Head of a Lady—pencils—(three)   3

41 Portrait of Mrs William Petrie, in frilled white dress and cap; and Portrait of a Lady, in white dress with green sash—(two)   2

42 Portrait of Miss Mary Tadman, in white Empire dress with pearl necklace—signed in full, and dated Novr 1809; and Portrait of a Lady, in white Empire dress, landscape background—(two)   2

43 Portrait of Miss Holland, later Mrs Crawford, in white dress—signed in full, and dated 1799; and Portrait of Mrs Peters—(two)   2

44 Portrait of Mrs Parker, of Bath, in white muslin dress, with a riband in her hair—signed in full, and dated 1797

45 Portrait of Miss Smith, in white Empire dress, with a veil on her head and a lorgnette in her blue sash—signed with initials, and dated 1809, and inscribed 'Miss Smith, of Shalden, near Alton, Hants'

46 Portrait of Captain Hayes (of the 'Melville Castle'), taking snuff; Portrait of Baker, quartermaster on board the 'Dutton'; and Head of a Gentleman—pencils and wash —(three)   3

47 Portrait of Colonel Maxwell, playing the violin—dated 1785; and Portrait of Mr Henchman—pencils and wash—(two)   2

48 Portrait of Captain Edward O'Brien; and Portrait of Captain O'Brien Drury— pencil and wash—(two)   2

49 Portrait of James Lucy Deighton, Esq.—signed with initials, and dated 1790, Madras; and Portrait of his brother, Richard—signed with initials, and dated 1790 I. —pencils—ovals—(two)   2

50 Portrait of Colonel Kidd, of Madras, in military uniform—pencil—signed with initials, and dated 1790, Madras—oval

51 Portrait of Captain Lambe, in naval uniform, seascape background—inscribed: 'Jno Smart delint 1795 on board the "Melville Castle", Captain Lambe'—pencil— oval

52 Portrait of the Rt Honble Lord Vis^t Duncan (1731–1804), Baron Camperdown and Viscount Duncan, the famous Admiral, in naval uniform wearing orders—pencil— signed in full and dated 1798

53 Portrait of a Brother of the Lord Elgin, probably Charles Andrew (1768–?), third son of Charles, 5th Earl of Elgin and 5th Earl of Kincardine, Governor of Prince of Wales Island

54 Portrait of General MacAlister, three-quarter face to the right in brown coat, white vest and cravat, with landscape background—in pencilled oval

55 Portrait of Master Petre, in jacket and frilled lace collar

56 Portrait of Admiral Sir Richard Onslow, Bart, in naval uniform, wearing an Order —signed in full, and dated 1798
  Sir Richard was present at the Battle of Camperdown on board the 'Monarch', as Divisional Commander to Admiral Lord Duncan

57 Portrait of Major Robson, Deputy Governor of St Helena, in military uniform— inscribed 'John Smart delint Septr 1795 St Helena'—pencil—oval

58 Portrait of Captain West, in blue coat and white vest and cravat, inscribed: 'of the "Dutton", Indiaman 1785 drawn on board going to Madras'

59 Portrait of Sir Archibald Campbell, in scarlet military coat with green facings, wear-ing the Star of the Order of the Bath
  Probably Sir Archibald Campbell, K.C.B. (1739–1791), Governor of Madras, 1786

60 Portrait of John Dighton as a child, in green coat and frilled muslin collar—signed in full, and dated 1804—the reverse inscribed: 'John Dighton aged eleven years born at Muticore (a hundred miles north of Madras), June 4th, 1793, and my Grandson and painted by me J. Smart'

61 Portrait of John Dighton, in blue coat, yellow vest and frilled white cravat— inscribed 'Portrait of John Dighton who died March 25th 1810 son of Lieut Col

John Dighton in the East India Company's Service and grandson of John Smart who painted this portrait a few days before his Death aged 17'

62 A Sketch of the Ship 'Consalateur', inscribed: 'Ship Consalateur, Monsr Bramont, Commander from Pondicherry to Port L'Orient: spoke with by Capt Jas West in the Ship Dutton the 1st June 1785. Lat 00.48 So. Lon. 24.15 Wt a London'

63 Portrait of John James Smart, as a child, in white dress trimmed with blue riband —signed with initials, and dated 1807—in oval pearl frame
John James Smart (*c.* 1806–1856), son of the artist by his second wife, Mary Morton[1]

64 Portrait of the Artist (1741–1811), nearly profile to the right, in grey-green coat, white vest and white cravat, his hair powdered—signed with initials, and dated 1797—in oval gold frame, the reverse with his monogram and a lock of hair

65 The Artist's Sketch Book, containing numerous studies of heads and various drawings of Tropical fish, touched with colour, etc.; and Four Prints, after Smart and Bowyer

66 An Oval Gold Miniature Frame, the reverse set with a medallion painted with classical figures within a seed-pearl border on a blue glass ground

67 Portrait of Mr Bayley, father-in-law of John James Smart, three-quarter face to the left, in dark coat with a white cravat—oval

[1] See family tree for correct dates.

Engravings after John Smart and J. Smart, Junior

ANDERSON, JAMES	L. Schiavonetti
BOYD, SIR ROBERT	C. Watson, 1785
BURR, DANIEL	R. Graves
CHESTERFIELD, 4TH EARL	Goulding Welbeck Collection, 1916
CLINTON, SIR HENRY	F. Bartolozzi, 1780
COCKBURN, THOMAS	Williamson, *History of Portrait Miniatures*, 1904
CORNWALLIS, 1ST MARQUIS	Williamson, *History of Portrait Miniatures*, 1904
GEORGE IV	L. Sailliar, 1788
KNIGHT, SIR J.	W. Ridley, 1804
LACEY, MICHAEL	Rophino, 1807
OAKELEY, SIR CHARLES	Williamson, *Pierpoint Morgan Collection*, 1906
OAKELEY, HELENA, LADY	Williamson, *Pierpoint Morgan Collection*, 1906
O'BRYEN, EDWARD	W. & J. Skelton, 1809
ROUT, MRS (aged 82)	L. Haghe
RUDDIMAN, WILLIAM	A. Cardon
STANHOPE, PHILIP	Goulding Welbeck Collection, 1916
TAYLOR, SIR J.	J. Dixon
WALPOLE, THOMAS	Williamson, *History of Portrait Miniatures*, 1904
WIGRAM, FAMILY	C. Turner, 1826
YOUNG, SIR G.	J. Blood, 1814

John Smart Junior

KEELEY, MARY }	P. Hoares, '*No Songs No Supper*'
LYGON, EDWARD }	

Engraving by J. Smart, Junior

JOHN SMART, JUNIOR, SELF PORTRAIT   (Not published)

Selected Sources of Reference

Bazaar Exchange and Mart, January 1937.
Busteed, J. W., family papers.
British Museum Catalogue of Engraved Portraits, Vol. VI, 1925.

Cansick, F. T., MS., Monumental Inscriptions (St Pancras Town Hall).
Chancery Court Proceedings, 1790.
Christie, Manson & Woods, Catalogues.
Commonwealth Relations Office, Public Dispatches 1784–8, Vol. 88.
Cotton, Mr, Tombs in Madras.
Coutts, Messrs, Bankers, London.

Dighton, C., *The Dightons of Clifford Chambers*, London, 1903.
Dossie, Robert, *Memoirs of Agriculture*, 3 Vols., London, 1767–82.

Farington. Joseph, *Diary* of, Windsor Typescript.
Foster, J. J., *Dictionary of Painters of Miniatures*, London, 1926.
Foster, Sir William, *British Artists in India*, Walpole Soc., Vol. XIX, Oxford, 1931.

Gentleman's Magazine, The, London, 1811.
Graves, Algernon, *The Society of Artists and the Free Society*, London, 1907.
— *The Royal Academy of Arts*, London, 1905–6.
— *A Dictionary of Artists*, London, 1895.
Greig, James, *Diary of Joseph Farington, R.A. Edit.*, London, 1922–8.
Grindon, family papers.
Gwynn, Stephen, *Memorials of an Eighteenth Century Painter*, London, 1898.

Hudson, D., and Luckhurst, K. W., *The Royal Society of Arts*, London, 1954.

Jaffé, Arthur, *The Art Quarterly*, Autumn, 1954.
— MSS., in the possession of the family.

Long, Basil, *British Miniaturists*, London, 1929.
Luckhurst, K. W., *William Shipley and the Royal Soc. of Arts*, London, 1949.

Madras Courier, Vol. XI, 1795.
Montgomery, Martin R., *The Indian Empire*, London, 1861.

Public Records Office.

Redgrave, Samuel, *A Dictionary of Artists of the English School*, London, 1878.
Reynolds, Graham, *English Portrait Miniatures*, London, 1952.

Royal Academy, MSS. on The Incorporated Society of Artists.

Smith, J. T., *Nollekens and His Times*, Edit. by E. Gosse, London, 1895.
Somerset House.
Sotheby and Co., Records and Catalogues.

Twining, Thomas, *Travels in India*, London, 1893.

Walpole Society, Vols. XXXII and XIX.
Williamson, Dr G. C., *Portrait Miniatures*, London, 1897.
— *Ozias Humphry*, London, 1919.
— *The Miniature Collector*, London, 1921.
— *The History of Portrait Miniatures*, 2 Vols., London, 1904.

Index

1. Richard Brompton (d. 1782)
John Smart, c. 1780
$30\frac{3}{4} \times 25\frac{1}{4}$ in.

PLATE I

2. Gilbert Stuart (1755–1828)
John Smart, c. 1783
24 × 20 in.

3. Lemuel F. Abbot (1760–1803) Attrib.
John Smart, c. 1800
35¼ × 27¼ in.

PLATE II

4. John Smart (1742/3–1811) Self Portrait, signed and dated 1783
$1\frac{1}{2} \times 1\frac{1}{8}$ in.

5. John Smart
Self Portrait (c. 1780–85)
$2\frac{3}{4} \times 2\frac{3}{8}$ in.

6. John Smart
Self Portrait, signed and dated 1802
$2\frac{3}{4} \times 2\frac{3}{16}$

7. John Smart
Self Portrait, signed and dated 1797
$3\frac{3}{8} \times 2\frac{3}{4}$ in.

PLATE III

8. Anna Maria Woolf, née Smart
(1766–1813) c. 1788
$3\frac{3}{4} \times 3$ in.

9. Robert Woolf (1755–1836)
Signed and dated 1786
$2 \times 1\frac{5}{8}$ in.

8A. Anna Maria Woolf, née Smart
(1766–1813) Signed and dated 1789. I
$1\frac{1}{4} \times \frac{9}{10}$ in.

10. John Smart, Jun. (b. 1762?
d. young) Signed and dated 1765
$1\frac{3}{8} \times 1\frac{3}{16}$ in.

11. John Dighton, Jun. (1793–1810)
Signed and dated 1804
$3\frac{5}{8} \times 3$ in.

12. Sophia Dighton, née Smart
(1770–93) c. 1788
$2\frac{4}{5} \times 2\frac{3}{5}$ in.

PLATE IV

13. Balgores House
(Now Gidea Park College)

14. Mary Morton (1783–1851)
c. 1804
$4\frac{1}{4} \times 3\frac{1}{2}$ in.

15. John James Smart (1805–70)
Signed and dated 1807

16. Portable sundial and compass
by John Gilbert, c. 1775
$4\frac{1}{4}$ in. square

PLATE V

17. Robert Woolf, Jun. (1786/7–1825)
Signed and dated 1796
6¾ in. diam.

PLATE VI

18. A herdsman playing his flute, signed and dated April
22nd, 1755. $7\frac{7}{8} \times 6\frac{1}{8}$ in.
Presented to Miss Smirke, 22 August 1850
Collection of Michael Jaffé, Esq.

PLATE VII

19. Pencil drawing
Signed and dated 1755
$14\frac{1}{2} \times 13\frac{2}{5}$ in.

20. An Unknown man
Signed and dated 1763
$1\frac{3}{8}$ in. high

21. Mrs Yates
Signed and dated 1761
$1\frac{1}{4} \times 1$ in.

PLATE VIII

22. William Jones, Esq.
Signed and dated 1764
$1\frac{1}{2} \times 1\frac{1}{4}$ in.

23. An unknown man
Signed and dated 1764
$1\frac{3}{8}$ in. high

24. Gore Townsend
Signed and dated 1767
$1\frac{3}{8} \times 1\frac{1}{4}$ in.

25. Eleanor Smart (afterwards Lady
Carteret) Signed and dated 1766
$1\frac{11}{16} \times 1\frac{7}{16}$ in.

26. Jane Hassell (afterwards
Mrs. Kemeys-Tynte) d. 1825
Signed and dated 17?, c. 1765
$1\frac{2}{5} \times 1$ in.

27. An unknown Man
Signed and dated 1769
$1\frac{1}{2} \times 1\frac{1}{4}$ in.

PLATE IX

28. James Bruce (1730–94)
Signed and dated 1776
1½ in. high

29. Viscountess Townshend, later
Anne, 1st Marchioness Townshend
Signed and dated 1775
2⅜ in. high

30. An unknown Lady
Signed and dated 1781
2 × 1½ in.

31. Sir Archibald Campbell (1739–91)
Signed and dated 1775
1⅓ × 1½ in.

32. Major William Davy
Signed and dated 1775
1¼ × 1 in.

33. An unknown Lady
Signed and dated 1774
2⅛ in. high

PLATE X

34. The Hon. William Cockayne
Signed and dated 1782

35. The Hon. William Cockayne
c. 1782
$2\frac{1}{5} \times 1\frac{4}{5}$ in.

36. An unknown Lady
(enamel)

37. An unknown Lady
(enamel) c. 1775
$1\frac{1}{2} \times 1\frac{3}{16}$ in.

38. An unknown Lady
c. 1782 (sketch for Fig. 40)

39. An unknown Lady
Signed and dated 1782

PLATE XI

40. Mrs. Ward, née Thomas
$2\frac{1}{2} \times 2\frac{1}{8}$ in.

41. Lady Emily Mary Salisbury,
1st Marchioness of Salisbury
Dated 1781
$2\frac{1}{2} \times 2$ in.

42. Lady Oakeley, née Helena Beatson
c. 1786
$2\frac{9}{10} \times 2$ in.

43. Miss Gascoine
c. 1775
$2\frac{1}{2} \times 2$ in.

PLATE XII

44. An unknown Lady
c. 1780
$2\frac{5}{8} \times 2\frac{1}{8}$ in.

45. Lieut. Gen. Sir Robert Boyd, K.B.
(1710–94) Signed and dated 1784
$1\frac{29}{32} \times 1\frac{3}{8}$ in.

46. Mrs. Thomas Lewin
Signed and dated 1784

47. Thomas Lewin, Esq.
Signed and dated 1786

48. Sarah Tyssen
Signed and dated 1781
$2\frac{1}{4}$ in. high

49. Lieut. Gen. Sir Robert Sloper,
K.B. Signed and dated 1787, I.
$2 \times 1\frac{1}{2}$ in. approx.

50. Mrs. Campbell, née Elizabeth
Mackay. Signed and dated 1787, I
$2\frac{1}{4}$in. high

PLATE XIII

51. Mr. Dog(h)arty and Dr. William Johnson
Dated 1785
$5\frac{1}{2} \times 7\frac{1}{2}$ in.

52. Baker, Q.M. of the *Dutton*
1785
$4\frac{3}{4} \times 4$ in.

53. Master Impey, 3rd son of Sir
Elija Impey. Inscribed and dated 1785
$3\frac{3}{4} \times 3\frac{1}{4}$ in.

PLATE XIV

54. Captain William Richard Rumbold
c. 1780
$2\frac{1}{4} \times 2$ in.

55. The Hon. Charles Andrew Bruce
4×3 in.

56. Mr. (Afterwards Sir Richard)
Sullivan. Signed and dated 1785
$3 \times 2\frac{1}{2}$ in.

57. H.R.H. Prince Henry Frederick,
Duke of Cumberland (1745–1813)
$2\frac{3}{4} \times 2\frac{3}{8}$ in.

PLATE XV

58. James Lucy Dighton, Esq.
Signed and dated 1790. I
6 × 5 in.

59. Robert, Baron Hobart, 4th Earl
of Buckinghamshire (1760–1816)
Inscribed and dated 1793
$5\frac{3}{4} \times 5\frac{1}{4}$ in.

60. An unknown man
$3\frac{3}{16} \times 2\frac{3}{8}$ in.

61. Sir Archibald Campbell, K.B.
Signed and dated 1788. I
3 × $2\frac{3}{8}$ in.

PLATE XVI

62. Muhammad Ali, Nawab of Arcot
Signed and dated 1792
$2\frac{1}{2} \times 2$ in.

63. Muhammad Ali, Nawab of Arcot
Signed and dated 1788. I
2 in. high

64. An unknown Indian youth
Signed and dated 1788. I
$2\frac{3}{16} \times 1\frac{11}{16}$ in.

65. An unknown Indian girl
Signed and dated 1790. I
$2\frac{1}{2} \times 1\frac{7}{8}$ in.

PLATE XVII

66. Sir Charles Oakeley, Bart,
D.C.L. (1751–1826)
Signed and dated 1786. I
$2\frac{1}{4} \times 1\frac{1}{2}$ in.

67. Lady Oakeley (1762–1839)
Signed and dated 1786. I
$2\frac{1}{4} \times 1$ in.

68. Charlotte Porcher
Signed and dated 1788. I
$2\frac{3}{8}$ in. high

69. General Colin Macaulay
(1760–1836)
Signed and dated 1792. I
$3 \times 2\frac{3}{8}$ in.

70. Mr. (later The Rt. Hon. Sir
William) Garrow
Signed and dated 1788. I
$2\frac{1}{4} \times 1\frac{11}{16}$ in.

PLATE XVIII

71. The Rt. Hon. Charles, Earl Cornwallis, K.G. (1738–1805)
Signed in full and dated 1792
$7\frac{1}{2} \times 7$ in.

72. Bronze Medallion
by C. H. Küchter
$1\frac{7}{8}$ in. diam.

PLATE XIX

73. Abdul Khalick, elder son of Tippoo
Signed in full 1794
$6 \times 5\frac{1}{2}$ in.

74. Mooiz Ud Din, younger son of Tippoo
Signed in full and dated 1794
$6 \times 5\frac{1}{4}$ in.

PLATE XX

75. Capt. Hayes of the *Melville Castle*
Dated 1785
$3\frac{3}{4} \times 3\frac{1}{8}$ in.

76. Miss Twining
Signed and dated 1801
$3\frac{3}{4} \times 3$ in.

77. Major Robson
Signed and dated in full 1795
$7 \times 6\frac{1}{2}$ in.

78. An unknown man
Inscribed 'Jno Smart' 1795

PLATE XXI

79. Flying Fish
1795
$4 \times 7\frac{1}{2}$ in.

80. Leopard Fish
1795
$4 \times 7\frac{1}{2}$ in.

PLATE XXII

81. A Young girl
2⅜ × 2 in.

82. A young girl
Signed and dated 1797
2⅛ × 1⅝ in.

83. Laetitia Burroughs, afterwards Lady Ogle
Signed with initials, c. 1797
2½ × 2⅛ in.

84. Miss Marianne Capper
Signed and dated 1788
1½ in. high.

85. Miss Darrell (called)
Signed and dated 1785
1⅝ in. high

PLATE XXIII

86. Sir Robert Wigram
Signed and dated 1805
$4\frac{7}{8} \times 4$ in.

87. Capt. Pultney Malcolm, later Vice-
Admiral, Sir Pultney Malcolm
Signed in full and dated 1809
$5\frac{3}{4} \times 5\frac{1}{4}$ in.

88. Dr. Reid
Signed and dated 1802
$3\frac{1}{8} \times 2\frac{1}{2}$ in.

89. An unknown lady
Signed and dated 1800
$3\frac{5}{8}$ in. high

PLATE XXIV

90. Mrs. Smart, née Morton (called)
Signed and dated 1806
3⅜ in. high

91. Master Betty (W. H. West Betty)
(1791–1874)
Signed in full and dated 1806
4⅛ × 3¼ in.

92. Patrick Colquhoun
Signed and dated 1807
2¾ × 2⅛ in.

93. Admiral John Wells, K.C.B.
Signed and dated 1808
3 × 2¼ in.

PLATE XXV

94. Joseph, Richard, Ely, Loftus and Elwood, sons of Sir Robert Wigram
$8\frac{1}{2} \times 6$ in.

95. Harriet, Eleanor and Anne, daughters of Sir Robert Wigram
$8\frac{1}{4} \times 7$ in.

PLATE XXVI

96. Colonel Reynolds
sketch for a miniature, d. 1810
Signed and dated 1809
5 × 4¼ in.

97. Mr. Holland (called)
Signed and dated 1806
3¾ in. high

98. An unknown lady
? a member of the Smart family
5½ in. high

PLATE XXVII

99. Miss Keating
Signed and dated 1811
6 × 4 in.

100. An unknown lady
Signed in full and dated 1810
4 × 3 in.

101. Col. Keith Michael Alexander
Signed and dated 1810
$3\frac{3}{8} \times 2\frac{3}{4}$ in.

102. Miss E. Anderson
Signed in full and dated 1810
$5\frac{1}{2} \times 4\frac{5}{16}$ in.

PLATE XXVIII

103. John Smart, Jun. (1776–1809)
self portrait
Signed in full and dated 1800
Inside oval $5\frac{5}{8} \times 4\frac{3}{4}$ in.

104. John Smart, Jun.,
by John Smart, Senior
Signed and dated 1808
$5\frac{1}{8} \times 3\frac{1}{4}$ in.

105. Robert Woolf, Jun. (1786/7–
1825)
Signed and dated 1805, J.S.J.
$5\frac{1}{8} \times 4\frac{1}{2}$ in.

106. Miss Mary Anne Green
Signed and dated, J. Smart, Jr. 1807
$4\frac{1}{2} \times 3\frac{7}{8}$ in.

PLATE XXIX

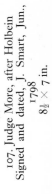

107. Judge More, after Holbein
Signed and dated, J. Smart, Jun.,
1798
8½ × 7 in.

108. An unknown lady, formerly
called Anne of Cleves, after Holbein
Signed, J. Smart, Jun., 1798
8¼ × 7 in.

PLATE XXX

109. Horatio Townshend
Signed and dated, J. S., Jr., 1801,
after J. Smart, Sen.
$2\frac{1}{2} \times 2$ in.

110. Miss Binney
Signed, J.S.J., 1807

111. The Hon. Edward P. Lygon
Signed and dated, J.S.J., 1806
$3\frac{13}{16} \times 3\frac{1}{4}$ in.

112. The Hon. Mrs. Walpole
Signed and dated, J.S.J., 1806
4 in. high

PLATE XXXI

113. Details of Annual Dinner of the Incorporated Society of Artists
Oct. 10th, 1770

PLATE XXXII